LEOPOLD & LOEB

MURDER OF BOBBY FRANKS

ALAN R. WARREN

Introduction by
JOHN COPENHAVER
Afterword by
JOHN BOROWSKI

Copyright © 2021 Alan R. Warren
All rights reserved.

All rights reserved. No part of this book may be reproduced, scanned, or distributed in any printed or electronic form without permission of the author. The unauthorized reproduction of a copyrighted work is illegal. Criminal copyright infringement, including infringement without monetary gain, is investigated by the FBI and is punishable by fines and federal imprisonment. Please do not participate in or encourage privacy of copyrighted materials in violation of the author's rights. Purchase only authorized editions.

House of Mystery Publishing
Seattle, Washington, USA
Vancouver, British Columbia, Canada
First Edition

Cover design, formatting, layout, and editing by Evening Sky Publishing Services

ISBN (Hardback): 978-1-989980-56-9
ISBN (Paperback): 978-1-989980-57-6
ISBN (eBook): 978-1-989980-58-3

CONTENTS

Preface	v
Introduction	xix

PART I
THE CRIME

1. The Couple That Kills Together, Stays Together	3
2. I'm Taking a Ride With My Best Friend	22

PART II
THE CONFESSIONS

3. The Confession of Richard Loeb	61
4. The Confession of Nathan Leopold	98

PART III
JUDGMENT DAY

5. Trial, Psych & Sentence	149
6. Jail, Death & Parole	186

PART IV
B-Side And Rareties

7. Chisel Bandit   203
8. Life After Death   207

Afterword   213
Timeline of Events   221
References   227
About the Author   233
Also by Alan R. Warren   235

PREFACE

Killer Queens is a new series of historical fiction books based on true stories. Sources, such as police reports and newspaper articles, are examined to gather as many facts as possible surrounding each case. As with any work of fiction, some creative additions are made when telling these stories, usually within the conversations between the personalities involved. The various sources are the basis of these conversations and hopefully, make them come alive for the readers to help understand what was meant by those words.

The *Killer Queens* series of books explores the world of murder in the gay community, whether the victims or the killers themselves and sometimes both, are homosexual. One of the most common questions in gay-related murders is: how are they different from heterosexual murders? This is an important question, as homosexuality was considered a criminal act for so many years.

If you were caught performing a homosexual act in the Victorian Era, they would say you were "sexually insane" and commit you to an insane asylum. By the early 1900s, most countries decided it was more of a deviant act, something you shouldn't do. They would put you into a regular prison instead of an insane asylum if you were caught. By doing so, homosexuality became a crime, not as severe as murder, but more on the level of crimes such as theft, burglary, or arson.

A stunning example of the treatment of homosexuals in society is that of Alan Turing. Turing was a British mathematician, cryptanalyst, and computer scientist during World War II. In 1939, he joined the Hut 8 team. There, he solved the German Enigma code, which was considered the turning point for the Allied Forces winning the war against the Nazis.

So, what did society decide to do with one of its heroes?

Alan Turing was a homosexual. In 1952 when he was 39-years old, he started a relationship with Arnold Murray, who was 19-years old. Shortly after the couple began seeing each other, Turing's house was robbed. After the police investigated the crime, they found out that the thief was Murray and that Turing and Murray had been acquainted. It was also discovered that the two men had been involved in a sexual relationship. Both men were charged with gross indecency. Turing later pleaded guilty to the charges and was convicted. He was given a choice between imprisonment or conditional probation.

What were the conditions he had to meet?

Turing had to undergo physical, hormonal changes designed to reduce his libido. He received several injections over one year, which feminized his body. During that year, he became impotent and grew breast tissue. Along with his body's changes, he had his security clearance removed and lost his job with the British Intelligence Agency. He tried to move to America, but they denied him as he was then a convicted felon.

On June 7, 1954, Turing committed suicide in his home by ingesting cyanide. His housekeeper found him the following day, with a half-eaten apple laying beside him in his bed. It was hypothesized that he had doused the apple with the cyanide. An inquest later determined that he had committed suicide.

When society forces one of its citizens to be sterilized for the reason of being homosexual, one considered to be among the best and a war hero, why would they care about other homosexuals who are being murdered or hurt?

It didn't end there.

Even after homosexuality was made legal in 1967, it was still considered a sickness or illness that needed to be cured in the medical community. Almost like alcoholism, only the general public looked at alcoholics with sympathy. After all, they were still good people, and it was just the alcohol that made them do bad things. It was the Christian thing to do to help them. Most alcoholics weren't even arrested for driving while drunk or starting a fight in a public place. They were merely told to go home and sleep it off; or, if they kept on fighting, put in the drunk tank by the police for a night.

Whereas, if you were having or attempting to have sex with someone of the same sex as yourself, you were a pervert. It was considered wrong, disgusting, dirty, and perverted behavior. It was also judged as something you didn't need to do. Why would someone want to have sex with another of their same sex?

The public didn't know what to do with homosexuals, not after they were no longer considered criminals or insane. At least with alcoholics and drug addicts, there were treatments for their problems, and after all, they just needed not to do it!

So, what would they do when they couldn't arrest these homosexuals or put them into the local mental institute?

History repeated itself, and they turned it over to the religion of the day. They believed they were successful in other cases with people they didn't understand, such as the Indigenous people of North America. To "civilize the savage," the church and state had their children forcibly extracted from the reserves they were imprisoned on and taken to Catholic schools so they could learn how to be "good Christians." Only now, many years later, an astounding number of unmarked graves are being discovered all over Canada, where Indigenous children were buried after their deaths at these residential schools. We do not even know the names of these children or why/how they died.

So, keeping up with societal tradition, Evangelicals developed a new program to cure homosexuals. It was called "Exodus." In other words, they intended to "Pray away the Gay." They convinced several young gay men and women that the devil's influence made them believe they were gay and that they could fix their "problem" if they turned their lives over to the Lord and worked through the Exodus program. If they did, not only would they be cured, but they would be able to live healthy, productive, straight lives. As with so many others of these religious plans to cure what didn't need curing, it left many young gays confused, in despair, and committing suicide.

A significant component of the books in this series will include an individual analysis of the killers. From the killers' outlook, was their reason for committing murder different because of their sexual orientation? In some cases, the question of who the murder was about will be examined – whether the murder was about the person they desired or the person at the heart of the murder. Or, was the murder about the act of desiring them?

The answer to this question is entirely different when the victims are also gay. After all, like any other minority group or class of people in the world, that fact in itself creates a reason for some to want to kill them. The sexual component is a very complex one, so it will take several examples to understand it.

Some cases involve both the killer and the victim being homosexual. In these particular cases, we can see quite a few similarities to that of heterosexual murderers. We will find emotional perspectives to be the major causes of the murders. The motive could be anything from jealousy to unreciprocated love or the actual murderer unable to find love due to mental issues or social circumstances. But most importantly, in all of those cases, the type of love, albeit homosexual or heterosexual, those being only the affections of such love.

BOOK ONE

In Book One of the series, we go to 1924 Chicago and follow the lives of Nathan Leopold Jr. and Richard Loeb. Both were from wealthy families and were very well educated. In fact, both were already attending university while they were still teenagers. But these two men would not end up being well known for becoming great doctors, lawyers, or inventors of some marvelous new item that everyone in America would have. They would instead become known for committing what would be labeled as the "Crime of the Century."

A unique part of this murder case was the relationship that existed between the two of them. They were known to be lovers at a time when it wasn't only illegal but unpopular amongst the conservative atmosphere of the country. At the time, there was a prohibition on alcohol throughout the 1920s and an increase in the popularity of religious mandates. This was mainly due to the perceived promiscuity of the younger generations.

Far more couples in America involved in a sexual relationship became commonly called "killer couples." But as usual, the press and majority of America never classified Leopold and Loeb in the same category of murderers - mainly because of their homosexuality. Followers of this murder case primarily focused on the fact that they were homosexual, and therefore evil. They jumped to the opinion that they killed because they were homosexual. They not only killed a teenager but a boy. Psychiatry was in its infant stages, and there hadn't been a lot of studies done in this area. And what was done was not accurate.

Looking back in time, almost one hundred years ago, we know better than simply analyzing this as a homosexual murder. There are so many more levels to this case than believed initially or reported. I don't think that it's a truth that these two only murdered because they were homosexual. The motive behind this crime was much deeper than this.

Quite often, when we get a couple that kills together, they each play a specific role in their relationship and the process they have in killing a victim. Often, after they are caught, one claims a lesser role in the crime. Such as with the Paul Bernardo and Karla Homolka case in Canada. After their arrest, Karla claimed that she was only participating in the murder of her sister because she was scared of Bernardo. He was the aggressor, the dominant spouse that controlled her.

In this case, it was believed that Loeb was the dominant spouse over Leopold. Though it may be true that one spouse is more assertive than the other, I believe the submissive spouse can learn to control their relationship over a period of time if they are clever enough to do so. In Leopold's case, he was assuredly smart enough to do this.

As their relationship developed, Leopold

started to set situations up for the two of them. Leopold learned how he could manipulate Loeb into doing what he wanted. You saw this happening more throughout the relationship. By the time the pair were arrested, Leopold was planning out everything the two would do each day. He knew what the outcome of their actions would be. This in itself doesn't make their relationship remarkably different from that of a heterosexual couple who was out murdering people. If anything, it proves that it wasn't about the particulars of their relationship and that they were two men having sex. It was about committing a murder.

The reasons many couples kill together can vary. It can be anything from a religion they both practice, a sport they both like to partake in, or even a fantasy one or both of them has. The key to understanding the murder lies in this detail.

Whatever their sexual proclivity is only becomes relevant if the murder is sexual. If the desire or reason for committing the murder is based on raping the victim, it becomes more relevant. But this was not the case with Leopold and Loeb. Not only were they not interested in having sex with the victim, but they also didn't care who the victim was. This fact was the unique characteristic of this couple's murder of young Bobby Franks. Their victim could have been anyone they came across that day. In most of the murders by couples that kill, the victim is known to them. Most likely, it's one of the primary reasons for killing them. In this case, knowing who the victim was going to be played no role in the murder.

This book is not trying to give you a final answer to this case. Its purpose is only to make you think about the many aspects that make up a murder case and its complexity.

Nathan Leopold was no angel as he described himself as a Nietzschean and believed himself to be a "Superman" who was above the law. However, unlike Richard, there was no evidence that Nathan put his beliefs into practice or contemplated doing so before he met Loeb. Leopold's fantasies centered around his role of using his 'superhuman' rights to protect his king. Unfortunately for Leopold, Loeb would fall in that role as his king. Leopold was a lonely, unattractive boy who was not very popular. So, when he caught the attention of Loeb, not only was he willing to do anything to have such a beautiful and popular friend, but he hoped to gain sexual interest from him as well.

Loeb reportedly did not share Leopold's sexual preference for men and quite often was in the company of several young and beautiful girls. But he was willing to trade sexual encounters for Leopold's help and involvement in pulling off various crimes.

The question was whether Leopold participated in the murder of a 14-year-old boy in an attempt to please Loeb and achieve his sexual favor, or was he active in the planning and initiating the murder to get Loeb to be his lover?

This scandalous murder was the inspiration for the 1929 play *Rope* by Patrick Hamilton, and in 1948, a movie by the same name was created by Alfred Hitchcock. In 1956, Meyer Levin, a classmate and friend of Leopold and Loeb wrote the book *Compulsion*, which also led to a movie in 1959 by the same name. Levin worked as a reporter for the *Chicago Daily News* and had published six successful books before *Compulsion*.

Leopold felt that Levin's book would threaten his possibility of getting out on parole from prison. He didn't want the attention in the media that such a salacious book would bring towards him. The first thing Leopold did was to bring a lawsuit against Levin, claiming that the use of his name would violate his parole.

Also in 1958, Leopold wrote and published his autobiography called *Life Plus 99*. In his book, Leopold never explained any of the details surrounding the murder itself. It was primarily to promote himself to the public and why he should be released from prison.

The press attacks on Leopold never stopped him from getting parole in 1959. But just after he was released from prison, he got some bad news. First, his lawsuit trying to stop the publication of Levin's book was rejected by the court. Then, he was told that they were making a movie based on this book.

Leopold then brought another lawsuit against the film, claiming that it would be an invasion of privacy and defame him in public to the point where he could not get employment or live a normal life.

The Supreme Court eventually ruled against Leopold on these charges, and the movie was permitted to go ahead with its production.

Great emphasis has been given to whether Leopold and Loeb were a gay couple. Though I do not believe this is too important of a question, I present the evidence we have about their relationship, demonstrating that it was more likely than not that they were gay. I don't consider the sexuality within their relationship to be relative. During the nearly 100 years since the Franks' murder, same-sex couples have lived in our society without murdering other people. The more important matter in question is to examine how they acted like a couple. They worked as a team to commit many crimes, from theft up until the murder of Franks. Like what we see in heterosexual killing team relationships, Leopold and Loeb had their roles within it. Throughout this case, we see dominance or control from one of the members, while the other plays a role in pleasing the other. Their sexuality in itself had nothing to do with it.

INTRODUCTION

JOHN COPENHAVER | CRIME WRITER

Consensual sex between same-sex couples wasn't decriminalized in the United States at the state level until 1962. It wasn't decriminalized nationwide until 2003 with the Supreme Court decision in Lawrence v. Texas. In particular, the idea of sex between men as a criminal act has been deeply ingrained in the United States, reaching back to the American Revolution, when "sodomy" was considered a capital offense in certain states. Viewing gay sex as a perversion of "normal" heterosexuality at best and criminality punishable by death at worse has created a misleading and long-lasting link between gay identity and criminality in our culture. Too often, we forget that, until recently, boldfaced homophobia wasn't the myopic prejudice of the few but rather the prevailing attitude of mainstream society.

Alan Warren's exploration of gay couples who have murdered in his *Killer Queens* series offers an opportunity to reassess notable cases, such as the murder of 14-year-old Bobby Franks by Nathan Leopold and Richard Loeb in 1924, by contrasting valid criminality, such as murder, with invalid criminality, such as same-sex sexual relations. The series is an opportunity to tease out how the historical moment – and perhaps the constant retelling of these crimes over time – has confused and conflated valid and invalid criminalities.

The vicious thrill kill of Bobby Franks was the bloody result of an intense and deeply unhealthy co-dependent bond between Leopold and Loeb. Yes, Leopold had a sexual infatuation with Loeb, and the two had sexual encounters. But the nature of those encounters had little to do with the usual mutual love and affection between gay couples. Instead, their encounters were a bartered reciprocity: Loeb permitted Leopold to act on his sexual urges with him in exchange for blind allegiance:

Leopold: "Just what exactly are you proposing?"

Loeb: "I'm not proposing anything, my dear. I'm just giving you the information on how you might get what you want."

"And just what is it that you think that I could want?"

"We both know what it is, what you desire. We just never talk about it."

"If that is the case, why would you think that I'd want it from you? After all, who wants it if it's not wanted as much by the giver?"

"This is what I'm telling you. If you want it from me, you have to stoke my passion to want to give it to you. Why don't you understand?"

"Passion should come from the heart, not the mind."

"Who decides this? Why does it matter what lights my fire, as long as it's lit for you when you want it?"

"Again then, what is it exactly that you are proposing?"

"When is it that you see me my most excited? When is it that you see such passion in my eyes?"

> *"Dear, I only see that when we are on one of your adventures."*

In this exchange, Loeb is laying out the rules for their relationship: *I'll permit sex* – "We both know what it is, what you desire." – *if you give me what I want*, which is, of course, partnership in his "adventures," the criminal expeditions that would eventually culminate in the Franks murder.

It's also telling that Loeb says, "We just never talk about it," when referring to sexual activity. Of course, it's not surprising that gay sex wouldn't be discussed openly in 1924, particularly among Chicago's wealthy elite, to which both Loeb and Leopold belonged. Not only was it criminal, but it was strictly taboo. By referring to gay sex without naming it, Loeb, who was usually considered the dominant personality in the relationship, reminded Leopold of the forbidden and shameful nature of his urges, all as a means for establishing leverage over him. He was at once humiliating and offering him the opportunity to express himself sexually, as long as he was compliant and helped him with his criminal activities.

One of the most compelling – and haunting

elements – to the Bobby Franks murder was what, on the surface, seemed to be a lack of motivation. Franks wasn't robbed or sexually assaulted, and Leopold and Loeb's connection to him was, at best, tenuous. So, why do this horrible thing? Even Leopold's own justification smacks of teenage excuse-making: he was like the Nietzschean Übermensch (Superman) who could operate outside the boundaries of morality because he was brilliant and exceptional and, basically, rules didn't apply to him. Even later in life, after he was paroled in 1958, Leopold still couldn't put his finger on the "why?" In his book, *Life + 99 Years*, he wrote: *"My motive, so far as I can be said to have had one, was to please Dick. Just that, incredible as it sounds. I thought so much of the guy that I was willing to do anything, even commit murder,"* which is an explanation that isn't an explanation.

In what Warren has assembled in the following pages, Loeb emerges as a master manipulator and violent sociopath, but Leopold's story is more complex – and more compelling. Prevalent mores of his times would suggest that his sexuality and his criminality were linked. After all, for much of the first part of the 20th Century, fear of the "aggressive" homosexual – dubbed "homosexual panic" – was employed by straight-identifying defendants to significant effect to justify their brutalization and murder of gay men. It's homophobic and wholly unsatisfying to suggest that Leopold was unhinged by his sexuality which somehow brought about a murderous impulse. However, the isolating homophobia of the 1920s may have eroded Leopold's sense of self and stirred up deep self-loathing, making him particularly susceptible to Loeb's machinations. He was a product of his environment, not an aberration of it.

Other murdering duos, such as teenagers Pauline Parker and Juliet Hulme, who bludgeoned Pauline's mother, Honoria Parker, to death in New Zealand in 1954, or Dick Hickock and Perry Smith, who killed four members of the Clutter family in Kansas in 1959, share similarities with Leopold and Loeb. In these cases, there was an intense and off-balance power dynamic complicated by homosexual desire. Like Meyer Levin in his novel *Compulsion*, based on Leopold and Loeb, writers take up and explore these cases in complex and compelling ways: The Parker case was immortalized in Peter Jackson and Fran Walsh's gorgeous film *Heavenly Creatures*, and Truman Capote transformed the Clutter murders into the greatest true crime novel of all time, *In Cold Blood*. In each of these retellings, the crime highlights a social concern larger even than the crime itself – the plight of the outsider – suggesting that these crimes weren't anomalous but rather products of the cultural attitudes of the times. A crime is easier to cast off if it's seen as isolated and atypical but much harder to wrestle with when it seems to be a kind of mislaid social commentary.

As you read the exploration of the case in this book, ask yourself: Would a young man like Nathan Leopold be as vulnerable to Loeb's manipulations today? If Loeb couldn't have harnessed and used shame to control Leopold, would he have been as successful at recruiting a criminal counterpart? Finally, to what degree can we hold the prevalent homophobia of this era accountable as a force to bear on this tragedy?

PART I

THE CRIME

1

THE COUPLE THAT KILLS TOGETHER, STAYS TOGETHER

Nathan Leopold was already in a bad mood, as he was frustrated that his "Brilliantine" brand of hair pomade didn't arrive, and he was left to use some common product purchased locally. Brilliantine, made by French designer Edouard Pinaud, was a product that people of his caliber not only deserved but required. It was a must-have if he ever wanted to attend a proper function or attend a dinner date.

Leopold spent hours dressing his hair with the expensive pomade, all while looking into the mirror and dreaming. He wore one of his three-piece solid-colored suits. He didn't go for the latest fashion that boasted bright, vibrant colors or patterns.

Leopold loved the soft feel of his hair as he ran his fingers through it and the delicious scent it permeated. It wouldn't be long before he drifted off into space, fantasizing that Loeb was standing beside him, and it was Loeb who was running his hands through his hair. Leopold had done this so often that he began to associate the scent of the pomade with Loeb.

Nathan Leopold Jr (r) & Richard Loeb (l)

This was the reason that he was so frustrated that day. He was going to spend hours driving with Loeb in the car without that attractive scent that always aroused him so much. Six hours would feel like six minutes.

Despite his poor frame of mind, on the evening of November 10, 1923, Leopold agreed to drive Loeb from Chicago to the University of Michigan. The drive would take around six hours one way, and they were going to burglarize Loeb's former fraternity, Zeta Beta Tau.

The total take ended up being about $80 in loose change, a few watches, some penknives, and a typewriter. It had been a considerable effort for little reward, which would also mean little sexual pleasure for Leopold as well.

When they were driving back to Chicago, there was complete silence in the car. Loeb tried to start a conversation several times, but Leopold would only give one-word answers. His responses were short and stark, with him using only one or two words. Loeb ignored Leopold's silence for the first hour as he was working the perfect crime out in his mind.

Loeb asked, "What's wrong, Babe?"

"You talk a lot and keep saying the same things over and over again. When I have nothing to say, my lips are sealed," Leopold replied.

"You love my way. I know that you do," Loeb answered back.

Leopold then blurted out, "I am tired of committing these useless crimes and therefore receiving little in return." *(Meaning affection.)*

Loeb knew that the only way he could break Leopold's silence would be to show him some affection. "You know what I require. It isn't a secret to you. You know that I love you, Babe.

There's no need for this behavior, this drama now."

While Loeb was working out details of his perfect crime in his mind, he stared out into the wilderness of the fields they were passing by. As he started to lay out his plan, he became frustrated that no press had reported on any of the crimes the pair had committed so far. Loeb wanted to commit the ultimate crime, or "crime of the century," as he would call it, that would have not only all of Chicago talking but the whole world.

Leopold was now analyzing Loeb's behavior. He was beginning to believe that Loeb was sexually insane – a popular term used throughout the Victorian age for those who could only get aroused or perform sexually in what was then considered normal. It was a catch-all phrase used to put people, mainly women, in an asylum if they didn't behave according to the moral standards of the time.

But this surely wasn't Loeb, Leopold kept saying to himself. After all, he had several girlfriends and always behaved properly. But why did he need to act in a criminal manner to perform with him? Was it that Loeb thought that man love was indeed a criminal act, just as stealing or setting fires to other people's property? If this was true, then what did Loeb think about him?

Suddenly, Loeb blurted out, "This is the day that your life will surely change. This is the day that things will fall into place. What could be more sensational than the kidnapping and murder of a child? If we demanded a ransom from the parents, so much the better. It would be a complex and challenging task to obtain the ransom without being caught. To kidnap a child would be an act of daring, and no one," Loeb proclaimed, "would ever know who had accomplished it."

But would such a crime be worth risking their freedom or even their lives? What would happen to them if they were caught? How could they and their families live down such a scandal? In Loeb's opinion, the police were not nearly clever enough to catch them. And frankly, the people that live in society deserved the criminals and crimes they had.

The decision to commit this crime or not eventually came down to the reward Leopold would receive.

Leopold: "Just what exactly are you proposing?"

Loeb: "I'm not proposing anything, my dear. I'm just giving you the information on how you might get what you want."

Leopold: "And just what is it that you think I could want?"

Loeb: "We both know what it is you desire. We just never talk about it."

Leopold: "If that is the case, why would you think that I'd want it from you? After all, who wants it if it's not wanted as much by the giver?"

Loeb: "This is what I'm telling you. If you want it from me, you have to stoke my passion to want to give it to you. Why don't you understand?"

Leopold: "Passion should come from the heart, not the mind."

Loeb: "Who decides this? Why does it matter what lights my fire? As long as it's lit for you when you want it?"

Leopold: "Again then, what is it exactly that you are proposing?"

Loeb: "When is it that you see me my most excited? When is it that you see such passion in my eyes?"

Leopold: "Dear, I only see that when we are on one of your adventures."

Loeb: "Exactly!"

Leopold: "But I don't want to be having love during a crime."

Loeb: "We don't need to have it during the crime. How many times has passion taken over your mind, so much so that you had almost no control over whatever else you were doing? Even without being with that person, your mind is completely absorbed in the passion."

Leopold: "Yes."

Loeb: "So, if you're to think of me, and when you've seen me in that condition, and what it is that we are doing, perhaps if you do that for me, I will share my passion with you."

Leopold: "How do we establish such a deal? How do you quantify it? When do I receive payment?"

Loeb: "Well, let's see. It should be based on the level of passion and desire that you permit to me. In the case of a simple, light crime, you would need to conduct, let's say, two or three crimes."

Leopold: "I need to be a little more assured on what I get and for what I do."

Loeb: "It's simple. You already know by now what excites me and how much each crime excites me, so plan accordingly."

Leopold: "Are you saying that it's the severity of the crime? Or the length of time that it takes?"

Loeb: "Both really. The severity of the crime will give you the amount of passion that I could share with you. And the length of time that the crime takes will guide you for how long I'm willing to give it."

Leopold: "That's interesting. What level of crime are you willing to accomplish?"

Loeb: "I'll leave that to you. After all, this is part of what creates my excitement – having you create a plan and propose it to me. The more evil the crime, the more excited I will be."

Leopold: "You'll go as far as I will suggest?"

Loeb: "Of course."

Leopold: "Would you like it if we did something evil to someone, rather than just their property?"

Loeb: "Now, you are understanding what I mean."

Leopold: "Perhaps kidnap, sexual assault, or even murder?"

Loeb: "Now, I am getting excited. Just you saying the words lights my passion."

NATHAN LEOPOLD JR.

Nathan Leopold Jr.

Nathan Freudenthal Leopold Jr. was born in Chicago, Illinois, on November 19, 1904. His parents, Nathan Freudenthal Leopold Sr. and Florence G. Leopold were very wealthy and well-connected to the Jewish community who immigrated from Germany. His father was successful in several businesses, including a shipping company, an aluminum can manufacturing company, and a paper box-making company.

His father was constantly traveling away from home for business, and his mother was bedridden with a virus shortly after Nathan had been born. Even though it was never talked about, Nathan felt responsible for his mother's illness. Nathan was primarily raised by his nanny, Mathilda "Sweetie" Wantz, a beautiful thirty-something-year-old from Germany.

Nathan was considered an above-average intelligence boy who spoke his first words when he was only four months old. But at the age of six, when he started to attend school, he was constantly picked on and teased as he was very quiet, clumsy, and didn't like to play sports with the other boys. His older brothers Michael and Samuel never wanted Nathan around. They were teenagers and more interested in finding girlfriends, so he would only be in the way. It also didn't help that his nanny was at the school gate at the end of every school day to walk him home, which embarrassed him with his classmates.

Around this time, it became known amongst the other servants of the Leopold household that Nanny Matilda was having sex with Nathan's seventeen-year-old brother Samuel. The affair continued for several years until Samuel found himself a regular girlfriend, and he stopped seeing Matilda. We later learned from Nathan that this was when he became smitten with Matilda and started to have sex with her as well.

His loneliness might have been why he became a great lover of birds. So much so that he would spend most of his day trying to understand them. He studied their behavior and habits and wrote notes about them. He constantly tried to understand how the birds communicated with each other and tried to figure out their language.

He would later publish two papers in the leading American Ornithological journal called *The Auk*. He was accepted into the University of Chicago when he was only fifteen years old. Leopold constantly bragged to his classmates that he had an IQ of 210, but there was never any proof of him taking the IQ test anywhere. A few of his friends were so used to him making up stories, so they didn't believe it.

When he entered the university, he was exposed to the philosophy of Friedrich Nietzsche, which later became his obsession. So much so that it would destroy his life. The philosophy fed into his ego as he figured that he was far more intelligent than his classmates or friends. He always tried to be the center of attention in any group setting. He believed that he should always tell others what was right and what was wrong. Even if they were discussing something that he wasn't interested in, he told them they needed to talk about another subject.

In 1924, Leopold started attending the Law School at the University of Chicago with dreams of transferring to Harvard Law School. His family had great expectations that he would become very successful in the legal world and even become a Supreme Court Judge.

RICHARD LOEB

Richard Albert Loeb was born to Albert and Anna Loeb on June 11, 1905, in Chicago, Illinois. His father, Albert, was a wealthy and successful lawyer and the retired Vice-President of Sears, Roebuck & Company.

Richard Loeb

Richard was a very outgoing, popular, and happy child interested in history and real crime stories. He loved history so much that he took graduate courses in the subject later in life when he was in university. He was an avid reader, and his family considered him very smart. So smart, in fact, that they enrolled him in the University High school, which was on the University of Chicago campus.

After starting at his new school, Richard began to show some manic characteristics that his parents considered a teenager's rebellious nature. Richard began to steal little things from other students, nothing expensive or even important to those he stole the items. The other students often didn't even notice or care about their lost items. They even told Richard about misplacing something and laughing about it.

Eventually, Richard was caught stealing a pocketknife from a classmate, and he quickly learned how to fabricate a story to cover his tracks. After that incident, he began to plan further thefts that he could be caught in to develop grand schemes to talk his way out of it. It was all part of his dream to become one of the greatest criminals of all time.

Richard graduated from University High School when he was only fourteen years old. He was then accepted into the University of Chicago.

It didn't go well for Richard at the University of Chicago because all the other students were older than him and weren't interested in being his friend. He ended up getting average grades for two years before he decided to transfer to the University of Michigan, where he could get a fresh start.

His grades didn't improve much there, but he became much more popular. He hosted several poker games and began to drink alcohol while studying his subjects. He also joined several groups, including the Discussion Club, where the students debated philosophy and politics quite vigorously. He also belonged to the Literary Club as he loved reading.

At the age of seventeen, he became the youngest person to graduate with a degree in History. He planned to attend the University of Chicago Law School.

THEIR RELATIONSHIP

When Leopold and Loeb met, it was during the summer of 1920. Even though the two of them had quite different personalities, they both felt an immediate bond. Just over three years later, in the fall of 1923, the pair reconnected after Loeb returned to Chicago from his time at the University of Michigan in Ann Arbor.

In the early 1920s, the bohemian neighborhood called "Tower Town" on the north side of Chicago started to become known as the gay district. Gay men from Chicago and all around the Midwest would go to the speakeasies and tearooms to socialize and feel safe.

One of Leopold's favorite places was called the Dil Pickle Club on Tooker Alley. He loved going there because they hosted group discussions or debates on same-sex activities, politics, religion, and philosophy. As Leopold always considered himself the smartest and most important person in the room, he became obsessed with winning the debate or having the final say on who the winner was. These group debates were probably the only real-life situations that he felt he was the one in charge.

PHILOSOPHY OF FRIEDRICH NIETZSCHE

To understand the whole meaning behind Leopold's Nietzschean "Superman/Overman" beliefs, you need to know a little about the philosopher who inspired him – Friedrich Nietzsche. Nietzsche's philosophy evolved over the six books that he wrote. However, one of his primary beliefs was about how unimportant the morality of humans was.

Many people believe their morals establish

their worth, not only in themselves but also in all others. This moral compass is used to rate the value of people. In Nietzsche's opinion, morality was worth nothing at all. Humans merely created values to make themselves feel important, but there was no real merit to be given to it.

Does it not seem strange that Leopold was wrapped up in this philosophy when he was gay? Of course, being gay was not considered a lifestyle or possible way of life in the early Twentieth century but an illegal act of bad behavior.

By believing in Nietzsche's philosophy, Leopold placed himself above others, i.e., he was superior to the masses. Or, as Nietzsche called it, "Ubermensch." Because of his self-proclaimed status, he was allowed to perform homosexual acts on others, free from moral guilt. He believed someone with his Ubermensch status couldn't commit crimes on those inferior to him.

This mindset led him and Loeb to pursue committing any crime that would come to their minds. The crimes they thought of, and did, were not for the purpose of the crime itself. So, when they decided to rob someone of their money or possessions, it was not because they needed the money or item they took. It was merely to raise them to a higher status among other Nietzscheans. This way of thinking allowed them to kidnap and kill Bobby Franks, the ultimate crime that would put them at the top of the pile.

They also believed that a young boy's kidnapping and brutal killing was not even a crime when you did it to the lesser of humans. So, there couldn't possibly be any type of punishment for it.

Both Leopold and Loeb were so immersed in this thinking that it allowed them to do what they did. The killing of Bobby Franks was only to raise their status, if only in their own minds, since nobody else, like Nietzsche, was watching to give them some sort of award.

Friedrich Nietzsche was not a popular philosopher when he was alive. In fact, quite the opposite was true. But he did gain fame among the Nazi Party within Germany. When Hitler was sentenced to five years in prison for attempting a government coup, he wrote his memoir, *Mein Kompf*, and it included many of Nietzsche's opinions. Hitler took them much further than anyone expected.

It was never ascertained how Leopold even caught onto Nietzsche. But it was known that Leopold was a strong follower of Hitler. So, it has been speculated that he learned of the philosopher through his support of and commitment to Adolf Hitler.

It is ironic, though, that the same philosophy Leopold used to accept his lifestyle would also be used later by Hitler to execute others that were just like him.

On Thursday, May 21, 1924, Richard Loeb and Nathan Leopold demonstrated to the world their Nietzschean superiority over the common people that lived among them in Chicago. After several practice runs committing minor property crimes, they thought they had the plans for the perfect crime. Only this time, it would be a major crime, one that would be committed without emotion or detection and would prove their status as Übermensch. The murder of 14-year-old Bobby Franks would be their vehicle.

Leopold had no objection to Loeb's plan to kidnap a child. In fact, he relished over the hours discussing and planning the crime during the previous winter of 1923. They planned to ask for a $10,000 ransom. That was enough to get the attention of the news media at the time and enough spending money for them to have fun, too, as neither of them needed any more money. How would they obtain it?

After much debate, Loeb came up with a plan they both thought was foolproof. They would tell the victim's father to throw an envelope containing the money from the train he was traveling on, going south of Chicago along the elevated tracks west of Lake Michigan. They would be waiting below in a car, and as soon as the ransom hit the ground, they would grab it and make good their escape.

That afternoon, the plan was put in motion, with Leopold and Loeb driving their rental car slowly around the South Side of Chicago on random streets, looking for a possible victim. By around 5:00 p.m., after driving around the Kenwood area for two hours, they were ready to abandon the kidnapping and try it on another day.

But as Leopold drove north along Ellis Avenue, Loeb, sitting in the rear passenger seat, suddenly saw his cousin, Bobby Franks, walking south on the opposite side of the road. Bobby's father, Loeb knew, was a wealthy businessman who would be able to pay the ransom. He tapped Leopold on the shoulder to indicate they had found their victim.

2

I'M TAKING A RIDE WITH MY BEST FRIEND

The morning of Wednesday, May 21, 1924, started just like every other day for the Leopold family. Sven England, the family's live-in driver responsible for taking the kids to school and the house servants shopping for food and other things, pulled the Willys-Knight car out of the garage to warm the engine up for Nathan, who would drive it to school.

After Nathan finished his morning classes, he would typically drive over to meet with Loeb, and they would usually go for something to eat and talk for a while. This Wednesday, there was a change in their plans as Nathan and Loeb drove downtown and parked. Leopold got out of the car and walked out of Loeb's sight to a car rental store.

Leopold rented the same car he had just driven downtown with, a Willys-Knight, only a dark blue instead of red. He paid $35 cash for the rental and claimed to be Morton D. Ballard. It was only about twenty minutes later when Loeb spotted Leopold driving his rental car past where he was parked, and Loeb started the car and followed Leopold to a restaurant on thirty-fifth Avenue. They both parked across the street and went in to have lunch.

The pair loved going out to eat, especially Leopold. He loved dressing up in his finest clothes and having people serve him great food and drinks. One of Leopold's favorite places was Joy Lo King, located at 11 W. Randolph Street, which sat a few hundred people. The waiters were all dressed in formal wear, and an orchestra played.

But ever since prohibition in 1920, these places had all become ghost towns. They weren't allowed to serve alcohol now, so the more sophisticated diners such as the Loeb and Leopold's families had to get their alcohol from illegal means and couldn't drink in public anymore. They now relied on their cooks to create special dishes, and they invited other well-off people over to try and impress them. They could only invite those they could trust, though, as it would be easy for them to get reported and have a big scene happen with the police.

After the pair finished their lunch, they walked back to their parked cars. Loeb reached into the rental car and closed all of the curtains before driving away. Leopold followed Loeb in his car until they reached Leopold's home, where they both parked in the driveway. Sven walked out and asked them if they needed any help. Leopold asked him to remove everything from his car and place it into the rental car. After Sven did that, Leopold asked him to fix his brakes as they had been squeaking a lot lately.

The pair got into the blue rental car, left Leopold's house, and headed to Jackson Park, which was located on the Southside of Chicago, and they parked. Jackson Park overlooked a Golf Course and a lake, so they sat there and waited for a possible victim to show up.

About two hours later, they decided to try another location. They drove towards the Harvard School and parked about a block away. The school had already finished classes for the day, and most of the students had already left the school grounds.

They noticed a baseball game going on in

the playground across from where they were parked. The players all looked to be freshmen or first-year kids, a perfect age for them to kidnap. They both focused on each player and paid attention to every detail to try and choose the ideal victim.

A few hours passed before the game ended, and the players were all starting to pack up their gear and head home. One of the boys leaving was an umpire who began to walk away alone. This caught both of their attention. He was a young teen, and he was alone. The pair quickly jumped into their rental car and started to follow the boy.

Leopold was driving and taking directions from Loeb. At first, they drove by the boy slowly to have a good look at him. The boy had his head facing down and seemed to be in deep thought as he never even noticed the car or them driving by. Leopold drove down the block, turned the car around, and headed back towards the boy.

Loeb claimed that he recognized the boy as Bobby Franks, a banker's son who lived in a yellow house just down the road from him. In fact, the Franks boy would play tennis on the Loeb family court sometimes.

As they pulled up alongside Bobby Franks,

Leopold slowed the car to a stop, and Loeb asked Bobby if he needed a ride. At first, Bobby refused the ride because he was only a couple of blocks away from his home. Then Loeb asked him to meet his friend Nathan Leopold. Bobby jumped onto the running board on the side of the car and said hello to Leopold. Loeb then started to ask Bobby about the kind of tennis racket that he used to play. Before he knew it, he was pulled inside the car.

As they traveled down 49th Street, while Loeb and Bobby talked, Loeb slowly reached under his car seat and grabbed the chisel he had there. The two continued talking while Loeb got the perfect grip on the chisel, which he needed to kill the boy quickly. Loeb patiently waited for that perfect moment, the moment that Bobby would turn his head so he could strike him quickly without Bobby knowing that it was coming.

Suddenly Leopold took a sharp left turn, which made Bobby look forward. Loeb reached around and grabbed Bobby's mouth with his left hand, and with a continuous movement, smashed Bobby on his head with the chisel. He quickly followed with a second blow, only this time even harder. According to reports later in the newspapers, it took Loeb several blows as Bobby remained conscious and kept fighting.

As Loeb continued to struggle with the boy, he stopped hitting him on the head with the chisel so that he could grab Bobby with both hands and pull him into the back seat with him. He quickly stuffed a rag down Bobby's throat and put a large strip of tape over his mouth. Bobby fell unconscious, and Loeb shoved him down onto the floor in front of his feet.

Loeb climbed into the car's front seat, and the two headed to the marshland near Wolf Lake that Leopold had discovered during one of his bird watching trips, and they stopped. Once they felt comfortable enough that there was nobody around, they stripped Bobby of his clothes. They knew that it was still too light to dump the body, so they decided to get something to eat.

While waiting for it to get dark, the pair were so excited they did nothing more than play with their food and say very little to each other during their dinner. They weren't stressed or had doubts about if they should have committed the murder. Instead, they were both running their fantasies through their minds.

Leopold anticipated what could happen that evening sexually between the two of them. He was sure this was going to be the most fulfilling event to occur in his life. He had finally fulfilled Loeb's ultimate dream, so now he was finally going to get the love that he had always wanted from the man that he had wanted for so long now.

Loeb's mind, however, was running the full replay of their perfect murder. He was fixed on listening to the struggle that Franks gave while in the back of the car. The replaying of the sounds he heard from Franks with each blow of the chisel sent chills down his spine. He could feel the hair on the back of his neck and couldn't stop smiling at Leopold.

When it became dark enough, the pair left the restaurant and headed to the planned location to dump the body. They parked and dragged Bobby's naked body from the car. As he lay on the dirty wet ground, Loeb poured hydrochloric acid on Bobby's face and genital areas, hoping it would make the body's identity hard to figure out if it was ever discovered. They then shoved his body into the drainage pipes found in the culvert and left to go home.

They had to make two stops before getting home: first, to call the Franks family to tell them that Bobby had been kidnapped, and second, to mail the ransom note they had written up. The

I'M TAKING A RIDE WITH MY BEST FRIEND | 29

rest of their way home, Loeb bragged about his planning and committing the perfect murder. This excitement only lasted until the next morning when Bobby Franks' body was discovered.

Meanwhile, in the Franks' home, Bobby's parents were sitting at the dinner table waiting for Bobby to return from his school and baseball game. Bobby's father, Jacob, was getting angry. Dinner was ready more than an hour ago, and he couldn't send his cook and servants home until they had eaten. Bobby's mother was upset as not only did she not like to have conflict within her house, but her oldest son, Jack, had been seriously ill with Chickenpox, and her daughter Josephine was restless and misbehaving.

Another hour passed before Bobby's father decided to call some of Bobby's classmates to see if he had gone to one of their houses after the baseball game. After he couldn't find Bobby at one of his friend's houses, he decided to head over to the school and check to see if Bobby was still there for some reason.

Right after he left to go to the school, the phone rang, and Bobby's mother answered. The man on the other end asked for Mister Franks. When she told the caller that he wasn't there, the caller told her that her son had been kidnapped. He informed her that Bobby was doing all right, and they would contact them again in the morning. He then hung up. Bobby's mother screamed and passed out.

When Mr. Franks returned from searching the school, he found his wife passed out on the floor. He revived her, and she told him about the phone call. Seeing that she was still distraught, he took her upstairs, and she laid down on their bed. He decided that it would be better not to call the police as he didn't want Bobby to get hurt.

When Leopold and Loeb arrived home at Leopold's house, they went inside to find his was father still up. So, the three of them talked for about an hour before his father went to bed. Leopold and Loeb went downstairs, and they had a few drinks, not talking much. About an hour later, Leopold drove Loeb to his house, and the two of them went inside and into Loeb's bedroom.

Loeb said, "Have I been asleep for all of these years? Was that magic?"

Leopold replied, "Your eyes are no longer

the same. They are eyes that I've never seen before, a stranger's eyes."

"I can't stop seeing the images in my mind, as if it's happening now! As if we are doing it at this very moment. I don't want it to end," Loeb admitted.

"I'm sensing something dangerous in you, very dangerous. What is it?" Leopold asked.

Loeb replied, "I'm just where you want me to be. I'm ready to be what you wanted me to be. Don't you see that? I'm primed. If you don't take it now, you won't get it. And you won't be happy."

Leopold walked over to Loeb, grabbed him, and kissed him intensely on his lips. He could feel the passion bursting from within Loeb. He could taste the danger on his lips, the same danger that he felt during the murder.

"Are you ready?" continued Loeb.

Loeb looked at Leopold in his eyes again and nodded yes. Loeb suddenly had a severe and stern look on his face and said, "Just don't forget who is wearing the trousers in this relationship."

The two of them started to laugh as they fell onto the floor, rolling around, embracing, and kissing. Before long, the two ended up in Loeb's bed, where after making love, Loeb almost passed out from the day's events.

As Loeb fell asleep, Leopold wondered if Loeb loved him or loved what they did together? Where was his love centered? Would they have to continue the killing to continue their love relationship? How could he ever really know the answer?

Soon he would have to get up and go home, but Loeb was the only love he had ever known. As he lay in his arms, he quietly whispered, "You're the only love. Soon I'll be gone, and I'll be dreaming about you. You're the only love this heart has ever known."

While the couple was still in their perfect murder dream cloud, little did they know that by the time they both woke up in the morning, that dream would be shattered, and things would fall apart.

The shattering started when a night watchman named Bernard Hunt found the chisel with tape wrapped around the bloodied blade in a ditch. He decided to keep it and turn it over to the police.

Jacob Franks was unable to sleep and decided to report the kidnapping of their son to the police in the middle of the night. Since he was a man of wealth and prominence in the city, he was seen by the Chief of Detectives Michael Hughes and Captain William Shoemacher.

By accident, a Polish immigrant, Tony Mankowski, was walking through the marsh at Wolf Lake where they had dumped Franks' body. As he walked by the culvert, he spotted the body. Suddenly he heard a rumbling on the railway tracks above him, so he ran up onto the tracks. He saw four signalmen riding on two handcars approaching where he stood. He yelled and jumped at them to get them to stop.

He took the four men down to show them what he had found, and they pulled the child's body out of the pipe in the culvert and realized that it was a dead child with no clothing on.

They figured that the kid had probably been out swimming with some friends. That's why he wasn't wearing clothes, and he drowned. His friends probably ran away scared. They looked around to try and find the boy's clothing but only found a pair of glasses.

Early the following day, the mailman approached the Franks' home and handed a servant who answered the door a special delivery letter, who then passed it on to Mr. Franks.

"DEAR SIR:

As you no doubt know by this time, your son has been kidnapped. Allow us to assure you that he is at present well and safe. You need fear no physical harm for him, provided you live up carefully to the following instructions and to such others as you will receive by future communications. Should you, however, disobey any of our instructions, even slightly, his death will be the penalty.

1. For obvious reasons, make absolutely no attempt to communicate with either police authorities or any private agency. Should you already have communicated with the police, allow them to continue their investigations, but do not mention this letter.

2. Secure before noon today $10,000. This money must be composed entirely of old bills of the following denominations: $2000 in $20 bills, $8000 in $50 bills. The money must be old. Any attempt to include new or marked bills will render the entire venture futile.

3. The money should be placed in a large cigar box, or if this is impossible, in a heavy cardboard box, securely closed and wrapped in white paper. The wrapping paper should be sealed at all openings with sealing wax.

4. Have the money with you, prepared as directed above, and remain at home after one o'clock. See that the telephone is not in use. You will receive further communication instructing you as to your final course. As a final word of warning, this is an extremely commercial proposition, and we are prepared to put our threat into execution should we have reasonable grounds to believe that you have committed an infraction of the above instructions. However, should you carefully follow our instructions to the letter, we can assure you that your son will be safely returned to you within six hours of our receipt of the money.

Yours truly,
GEORGE JOHNSON
GKR"

Mr. Franks' attorney told him to go to the bank and get the money he needed to pay the ransom, and he would call Michael Hughes, the Chief of Detectives. Franks went to the bank and got the money just as the letter asked him to, in $20 and $50 bills, totaling $10,000.

The morning newspapers all reported the drowning of a young boy in a culvert near Wolf Lake and the kidnapping of another young boy from a wealthy family in the city. The Franks family or police did not yet connect the two stories.

In the following days, the Franks' offered a $5000 reward for any information leading to the kidnapper's capture. The Chicago newspapers, *The Tribune*, *The Herald*, and *The Examiner* also offered to pay $5000 each for any exclusive information on the kidnapping of Bobby Franks.

The police had the ransom letter examined by typewriter expert H.P. Sutton, who identified the Underwood as the typewriter used to write the letter. He also claimed that the person typing the letter was not a good typist and probably used two fingers. It was suggested that the writer of the envelope that housed the ransom note was an accomplished one who had tried to disguise his ability by printing poorly.

Joseph Springer, the coroner who performed the autopsy on Bobby Franks, described the wounds found on Franks' head as *"a small and sharp wound that was three-quarters of an inch long on the right side of the head near the hairline. A second wound which is about a half-inch long on the left side of the head also near the hairline. Both appeared to be downward blows."*

Springer also found bruises and swelling on the back of the head caused by some blunt instrument. When they opened up the scalp, they found a large amount of blood in the tissues. The cuts were sharp and very close to the bone. They were caused by some blunt instrument or weapon.

The coroner also found long superficial scratches running from the buttocks to the shoulders on both sides, suggesting the body had been dragged for some distance along the ground, probably without any clothing on.

Almost the whole face was discolored, probably by some sort of irritant being poured over it. This discoloration extended down into the windpipe, the right lung, and to the diaphragm, likely caused by the absorption of fumes.

The final cause of death was an injury to the head associated with suffocation, probably caused when a rag was shoved down his throat and taped over by the kidnappers. It was also concluded that Franks was not sexually abused during the attack; therefore, it was probably not done by a pervert. The time of death was estimated to have occurred within two to five hours before the examination.

On the afternoon of Sunday, May 25, 1924, the Franks family held a small service for son Bobby in their home. It was attended by the family, a few close friends, and twenty of Bobby's schoolmates from the Harvard school which he attended. At least twelve uniformed police officers were in the front of the house trying to regulate the over two hundred spectators, and press gathered there.

The service was conducted by the Fifth Church of Christ, Scientist. This was part of the Christian Science Network, which believed that the power of prayer could heal people's sickness. They didn't believe in the secular medical practitioner but instead had their own healing practitioners. Bobby Franks was placed in a white coffin with a blanket of crimson rosebuds.

After the service was completed, six motorcycle police officers accompanied the body to the Jacobs mausoleum at the Rosehill cemetery.

The *Chicago Tribune* discovered that the kidnap letter mailed to Jacob Franks bore a remarkable similarity to one that had appeared in a story called "The Kidnap Syndicate" in the May 3 issue of *Detective Story Magazine*. The discovery suggested to police that the kidnappers were probably fans of detective magazines.

The fictional kidnap letter read,

"Your wife is in our custody, and, so long as your conduct toward us warrants, she shall be treated with every courtesy and respect and, in so far as the circumstances permit, will be made comfortable. Any change in this attitude will be the result of your own defiance to our terms which are: That you make no appeal to the police or to any private detective agency. In that event, the amount stated below is automatically doubled, and let us assure you, it will avail you nothing and only bring great anguish to yourself and your wife.

Upon receipt of $50,000 in bills of $10 and $20 denominations delivered at the place, the time, and under the conditions which you will receive later, Mrs. Griswold will be returned to you within a very few hours thereafter.

> *Acceptance of these terms is to be conveyed to us as follows: You will leave your home tomorrow morning wearing a white carnation on the lapel of your coat and wear it all day. Following this, we shall send you further instructions as to how, when, and where the money shall be paid.*
>
> The Kidnap Syndicate

THEORIES

HAZING OF BOBBY FRANKS

On the day that Bobby Franks' body was discovered, Chief Detective Michael Hughes reportedly advanced the theory that Franks had been hazed. He learned from speaking with witnesses that Franks had been the umpire at an after-school baseball game and was kidnapped and murdered just hours before. Witnesses claimed that the team that lost the game had blamed their loss on the umpire's bad calls during the game. Hughes thought it was possible that Franks might have died by accident while they were subjecting to rough horseplay after the game.

. . .

POISON

When the Franks' body was discovered, there were noticeable brown stains around his mouth and a copper discoloration in his mouth and lungs. So, at first, detectives thought the boy might have been poisoned. Two of Franks' teachers were questioned by police, and one of them, Fred Alwood, the chemistry instructor, was taken into custody for a few days. Alwood was suspected of causing Franks' death by poisoning him because he had been at the Franks' home early on the night that Bobby had been kidnapped. Shortly afterward, Mrs. Franks received the phone call telling her that the boy had been kidnapped. Eventually, Alwood was released.

JOINT KIDNAPPING?

A 17-year-old girl named Gertrude Barker was reported missing to the police on Sunday, May 23, and had been missing since the same date that Bobby Franks was. The police believed that she was kidnapped by the same people that kidnapped Bobby Franks and perhaps even seized jointly.

Barker was last seen in the same location as Bobby Franks was at Ellis Avenue and 49th

Street. She left school at about 5 p.m., the same time that Bobby Franks left the baseball game. The place and time that the two disappeared were identical. Barker's aunt feared that Gertrude might have seen what happened to Bobby Franks and was also taken by the culprits.

Gertrude Barker was a quiet and shy girl who came from her parents' home in a small town in Washington State to go to school in Chicago, where she stayed with her aunt, a nurse there. According to her aunt, Barker had no boyfriends and had barely made any friends at school yet.

Later, Barker was found unharmed. She had taken a job in a horse stable where she was given an apartment in which to stay.

MORON THEORY

The moron theory was by far the most talked-about theory of why the Franks' boy was kidnapped and killed. Police were dispatched throughout the city looking for men arrested and brought before a court on charges of a similar nature. Moron murders had been frequently reported in the news, often around that time.

The key evidence for this theory was a pencil and paper found in the basement of a building still under construction and located next to the Harvard School and the baseball field that held the game on Franks' last day alive. The words "Robert Franks' pencil" were written on the paper, and the paper was wrapped around the pencil.

When Sergeant Powers searched the building where the pencil had been found, they found a boy's clothing buried in a pile of sand. Bobby Franks' body was found nude, so it was only natural to assume that the clothes belonged to him.

Detectives on the case figured that whoever kidnapped and murdered the boy removed his clothing and buried it in the construction site. The site was far away from where the body was dumped, so there would be nothing on the body to identify him.

DRUG ADDICTS THEORY ADDED, AND PERVERTS THEORY DROPPED

After a document was leaked from the State Attorney's office, they would have to explain this theory to the press: *"It is apparent from the investigations thus far that the killing of the Franks' boy was not accomplished by professionals. The professional criminal would not take such chances. He would not kill a boy and then undertake all the foolish risks of sending letters, making telephone calls, and sending taxicab chauffeurs on wild goose chases. If a professional had killed young Franks, he would have disposed of the body and fled. He would not have spent his time in contriving fanciful hoaxes."*

He also dropped the "Pervert Theory," *"It is not to be considered tenable that the boy's attackers were perverts. They would not have bothered about sending letters and chauffeurs to complicate the matter. I have discussed this phase with eminent psychiatrists, and they tell me that this type of crime is most likely to have been committed by amateurs in great need of money."*

He then continued to explain why he thought that it was drug addicts behind the kidnapping and murder, *"We shall, by a process of elimination, try to find someone, a user of drugs, who was sufficiently well acquainted with the habits and movements of the Franks family to have contrived a kidnapping plot. That someone would not have attempted the crime himself. He would have engaged someone else to do it for him. The killing was an accident, and everything that followed was undertaken to cover the accident. Dope will be found at the bottom of it all."*

WINSTON CAR - MISTAKEN IDENTITY

Joe Klon was driving from his home along

Chicago Avenue to work when he was spotted by two bystanders walking on the sidewalk. They noticed that he was driving a Winston vehicle just like the one reported in the news; that was the car that the kidnappers of Bobby Franks used.

They hailed down a patrolman, Thomas J. Foley, driving on the same road, only traveling in the opposite direction. Foley immediately chased down the Winston vehicle Klon was driving, stopped him, then took him into custody. The two bystanders caught up to Foley and Klon and accompanied them to the police station, hoping to claim the reward for finding who they thought was the Franks' murderer. The two bystanders were so excited about their capture that they both kept telling everyone at the police station, whether they were police officers or others being booked, that they had caught George Johnson, the killer of the Franks' boy.

Patrol officer Foley pointed out to the detectives that the guy he just brought in, Joe Klon, was not only driving a Winston, but he was wearing tortoiseshell-rimmed glasses as well. Klon got angry and snapped at the booking officers, *"This has got to stop somewhere. I'm going to have that car painted black or trade it in for a different type of car. I've got to wear glasses to see, but I'm going to* do away with those tortoiseshell-rims. This is the third time I've been arrested for murder in as many days."

This quick arresting of people who owned a Winston car or Corona typewriter was becoming a regular occurrence now. On Friday, May 30, 1924, four arrests were made for this reason: Porter and Ruth Ellis for owning a Winston car, Roderick Wolfe for having a matching typewriter with a letter still in the typewriter addressed to his wife saying, *"Tell Rodney not to get caught. There is a job for him in Louisville,"* and Miss Margaret Smith for only having a Corona typewriter.

TWO LETTERS AS TIPS

One letter was sent to Jacob Franks, father of the slain boy Bobby, insulting the father and threatening his daughter, Josephine's life. Jacob Franks' friend and attorney Samuel Ettelson were at the Franks' home when the letter was received. He called the State Attorney's office to report the letter and threat, and eight police detectives were assigned to watch the Franks' home.

Ettelson made a statement for the family, *"A letter addressed to Mr. Franks and purporting to be from the kidnappers was received this morning. It threatens the members of the family with death unless the investigation of the boy's disappearance and death are discontinued. We expect developments. A short time before the letter was received, a woman called up, and I spoke to her. She told me she had been living with a 'confidence man' whom she suspected might have engineered the plot to steal the boy. She said he had spoken to her a number of times about kidnapping and that one time she understood he was mixed up in such an affair. She said she left him because of his actions. She said he also was in the habit of having various poisons around their home and that he had been frequenting a poolroom at 63rd Street and Cottage Grove Avenue. The woman gave me her name and also that of a man. We will not make these known until we have investigated the information. She told us that he had a typewriter."*

The Franks' home had been inundated with calls and letters giving them tips to help solve the crime and threats to the family, usually to the father in particular. They also had an officer assigned to answer all the phone calls to determine which ones were worth taking note of and following up on. Among the threats were some threatening to bomb the Franks' residence, which the police believed and later set up a road check on Ellis Avenue where the Franks' home was located. They would scrutinize every vehicle that attempted to drive their road.

Police took this letter very seriously. Not so

much for the threat on Josephine's life, but because they figured it was written to cause a delay or disruption in the investigation of the murder.

A second letter was sent to the Chief of Police, claiming to be written by the killer of Bobby Franks. The person writing the letter said that they were sorry it happened and couldn't live with themselves anymore. Therefore, they were going to commit suicide. At first, they took this note seriously until tests on the letter proved that it was not written on the same typewriter as the ransom letter.

On Monday, May 26, 1924, a man named Lee Bugee, who was staying in room 1126 at the Hotel Sherman, had given himself some poison. Detectives immediately thought that it must be the kidnapper of the Franks' boy and rushed to the hotel. When they arrived at the hotel room, they found a poker game going on. The letter had been a practical joke.

FATHER'S REVENGE

These facts led to a theory that perhaps the killing was some sort of revenge on the father, Jacob Franks, a pawnbroker years before he became a millionaire. During that time, he was known as "Honest Jake."

Another letter was written on ruled paper and written in ink. It was written in the crudest manner of penmanship and was unsigned.

"You couldn't keep your dirty mouth closed. Well, we will go a little further, so watch yourself. To hell with the police. Those that are being watched and questioned are innocent, so watch her, Josephine. She is next. Bah, so you are smart, give your fortune to save your boy why you stingy cur. You could have saved him, but you are money mad. If I had you here, I would strangle you to death. Now you are crying. You made your money. Honest, haha. Honest Jake, but this world don't know you, but you shall suffer minute by minute. So, now every time you disobey us, we will strike. Go ahead."

A few days later, Jacob Franks made a statement to the press about his possible connection to the killer. *"They are persons Robert knew. They are persons I know. I have been racking my brains trying to think who they could be. Robert knew the murderers. That is why they choked him to death.*

Whoever it is that kidnapped my boy did so for the ransom. It was the money they were after.

They knew his habits. They knew my love for him and that I would willingly pay any sum to have him back. But Robert recognized them, and they grew afraid, and strangled him. They tell me I bear up under the strain very well, but they do not know.

I know it will not help that baby any to keep brooding. I try to put things out of my mind, but they come back. My wife keeps showing me the pictures of him. And I lie awake until dawn thinking about it all, thinking about that baby."

Robert was always considered "Baby" to his father and mother.

He continued his statement about his wife, Bobby's mother, *"She would tiptoe into Robert's room three or four times a night. He would not wake when she came in, but she would not be able to resist kissing him. Then he would rouse and throw his arms around his mother's neck, and they would hug each other. His sister Josephine was planning on going to Waverly College, but I don't think her mother could bear to have her away from home now."*

He was then asked about his wife's brother, Freddy Gresheimer, who had been brought into the police precinct and questioned about the murder case. *"It could not be he, but it is someone I know. But I cannot think who. As far back as I remember,*

I have never made an enemy. I was born in New York, but my father, who was in the tailoring business, came to Chicago when I was about six or seven years old. After grammar school, I started working at $2 a week. I suppose you could say that when the boys asked me for an increase in their allowances, I always told them how hard I had to work to get what they got for nothing."

The focus of the police and the press was on his time that he was a pawnbroker even though it was thirty-three years before, and he only did it for two years. Franks thought that that part of his life was being overemphasized.

On Sunday, May 25, two policemen from the Eight District went to the Leopold residence to ask Nathan some questions. Nathan had been sleeping when they arrived and felt too tired to get dressed, so he appeared in front of the officers, still wearing his pajamas.

The detectives wanted to know if he wore glasses, and Nathan responded that he occasionally did. Instead of asking him to show them the pair of glasses he owned, they asked him about the group of bird watchers he belonged to and if they frequented the Wolf Lake area to study birds often. After Nathan told the officers that the group had spent a lot of time at that park, they asked him to come to police headquarters and write a statement.

Later at the police station, Nathan wrote and signed a statement that listed his fellow bird watchers and the times he could remember going to the park with them.

"I have been going to the general locality of 108th Street and Avenue F for six years. I have been in the locality about five or six times this year. The last two times were Saturday, May 17th, and Sunday, May 18th. On May 17th, George P. Lewis and I drove out through the forest preserve and down south along the east shore of Wolf Lake to about 126th Street.

We then returned, arrived about 2:30 p.m. and left again about 5:00 p.m. Sunday, May 18, at the conclusion of a day's birding, Mr. Sidney Stein, Jr., George Lewis, and I drove along the road to the forest preserve and out to May's shack between Wolf and Hyde Lakes. We arrived about 6:30 or 6:45, walked east to the icehouse, back to the railroad track, and left by the same road about 7:20 or 7:30.

The purpose of all these trips was the observation of birds."

The detectives had to check over 54,000 records, which at the time were all manually written out, to find out who had purchased the pair of glasses found with the Franks' body. They were Bobrow horn-rim glasses sold by Almer Coe.

Glasses found at the crime scene

The first pair was bought by a judge and author named Jerome Frank, the second pair was purchased by a woman whose name was not listed, and Nathan Leopold Jr. purchased the third pair sometime in November of 1923, where he paid $11.50 for them.

After this discovery, the State's Attorney Crowe asked the police to bring Nathan in for questioning again. The detectives arrived at the Leopold residence and again asked Nathan if he wore glasses, what kind of glasses they were, and where he had them. He told them that he did wear glasses but not very often. And that he had somehow misplaced them and couldn't find them. The detectives didn't spend any time searching the residence, maybe because it belonged to a very prominent family, so they took Nathan to the precinct.

They confronted Nathan with the pair of glasses they discovered near the Franks' murder scene and asked if they were his. He was very coy with his answer telling them that the glasses sure looked like his, but he knew they couldn't be as his glasses were somewhere in his home.

Later that evening, a group of police detectives accompanied Nathan back to his house to search for his glasses, including Nathan's brother Michael. After about one hour, they were unable to find any glasses. That's when Michael suggested that perhaps Nathan lost the glasses at Wolf Park when he was out bird watching one night. However, Nathan agreed that the glasses were probably, in fact, his.

Nathan's admission concerned the detectives enough to ask him where he was on the day of the murder. In the beginning, he couldn't remember anything special about that day. Therefore, he couldn't tell them. It took them more than an hour of stern questioning to get Nathan to start to remember what he did on that day gradually.

He told them that he and his friend Richard Loeb had gone for lunch at the Marshall Field's Grill, and after that, they drove to Lincoln Park to look for birds. They had brought some alcohol with them and drank that in the park, which made them both 'happy,' he explained, but not drunk.

Then they went for dinner at the Coconut Grove Restaurant to help sober themselves up before they would head home, as neither of their parents would accept such behavior from them. On their way home, they came across two girls walking on sixty-third street who asked them for a ride. They eventually went to the park and had a few drinks with the girls they had picked up. A short time later, the girls decided to leave after one of them argued with Loeb. Loeb was supposed to go back to his house, where his aunt and uncle visited his parents, and drive them home. Once he told the girls they would have to wait for him maybe 45 minutes to do that, they left.

He told the officers that he thought the girls' names were Edna and Mae but didn't remember if he knew their last names. They questioned Nathan in detail about the two girls, but he couldn't remember much about them.

They next asked him if he owned a typewriter, and if he did, what brand was it. He told them that he owned a Hammond Multiplex for a few years, and before that, he owned a

Corona. When asked if he knew who Bobby Franks was, he said he didn't know him but knew of the Franks family.

Detectives then asked him if he knew much about the case or had followed it in the newspapers. He mentioned that he had followed the case in the papers and even read the ransom note there, and he figured the person that wrote it must have been educated. He also thought that the kidnapper must have known the area where the body was dumped; otherwise, there's no way that he would have been able to find that culvert at night in the dark.

During the interrogation, the detectives sent the police to the Leopold residence to retrieve the Hammond typewriter that Nathan admitted to owning, to compare its typing to the typing on the ransom note.

The typewriter that wrote the ransom letter

I'M TAKING A RIDE WITH MY BEST FRIEND | 57

Later that morning, they arrested Nathan and sent officers to pick up Loeb and bring him in for questioning. Before Loeb's arrival to the precinct, the press was somehow notified and waiting for him. The story was now out there about the two main suspects of the Bobby Franks kidnap and murder and that they were from two of Chicago's finest families.

PART II

THE CONFESSIONS

3

THE CONFESSION OF RICHARD LOEB

Crime scene where Bobby Franks body was discovered

On May 31, 1924, Richard Loeb made his confession to the kidnapping and murder of Robert Franks. The questions were asked by the Assistant State Attorney John Sbarbaro and Captain William Shoemacher on Saturday, May 31, 1924, at 4:00 a.m. at the office of the State's Attorney of Cook County, Chicago, Illinois.

Assistant State Attorney John Sbarbaro:
Q. State your full name.
Richard Loeb: A. Richard Albert Loeb.
Q. Where do you live, Mr. Loeb?
A. 5017 Ellis Avenue.
Q. What is your occupation?
A. Student.
Q. Where are you a student?
A. University of Chicago.
Q. How old are you?
A. Eighteen.
Q. You know that you are in the office of the State's Attorney of Cook County?
A. Yes.
Q. And you want to make a statement of your own free will?
A. Yes.
Q. Calling your attention to the 21st day of May, just tell us in your own words if

you know of anything unusual relative to the disappearance of Robert Franks?
A. On the 21st of May, Leopold and myself...
Q. What is his full name?
A. Nathan Leopold Junior and myself intended to kidnap one of the younger boys from Harvard school.
Q. Where had you planned this kidnapping?
A. You mean what?
Q. Where had you discussed it first?
A. Oh, I don't know. I don't remember. I don't remember when it first came up.
Q. Well, approximately, how long before the 21st day of May had you discussed it?
A. Oh, a month and a half, I would say, or two months, a month and a half or two months.
Q. All right, go ahead.
A. It was broached. The plan was broached by Nathan Leopold, who suggested that as a means of having a great deal of excitement, together with getting quite a sum of money.
Q. And adventure, as you would say?
A. Yes. We planned the thing quite

carefully. Every detail was planned. His car…

Q. What kind of car does Nathan Leopold have?

A. A Willys-Knight sport model. Red in color. His car is very conspicuous, and for that reason, we deemed it inadvisable to use it and therefore decided to get a car, rent a car from the Rent-A-Car people. Also, in view of the fact that such a car, if obtained under a false name, would not be incriminating were it to be discovered in connection with the crime.

Q. So, what did you do in connection with the car?

A. So, in order to assume a false name and a real identity, we went, and Leopold deposited $100 at the Hyde Park State Bank under the name of Morton D. Ballard from Peoria. Following out the same plan, I went down to the Morrison and registered under the name of Norton D. Ballard, carrying with me a suitcase, an old suitcase containing some books.

Q. Where did you get the books?

A. From the University of Chicago library.

Q. And for the purpose of taking those

books in that suitcase to the Morrison Hotel was to lead them to believe that you really intended to live there?
A. Yes.
Q. And had some clothing of some kind?
A. Yes. We addressed several letters to the Morrison hotel under the name of Morton D. Ballard.
Q. So that you might receive them?
A. So that we might receive them, and on the following day, I went and got those letters.
Q. That is, you would call for those letters on the following day?
A. Yes, the day after that, and I am practically certain that is what it was. It was the third day, the day after we went, pardon me, down to the Rent-A-Car people.
Q. For the purpose of fixing the time, that was about when?
A. Eleven o'clock in the morning.
Q. I mean, about the 20th day of April?
A. Yes. I am not sure of the time; I mean the date. I wouldn't swear to that. The 20th of April, how long is that?
Q. Just about a month before.

A. Yes, about a month. Leopold went in alone with $400 in his pocket, which I had drawn from my account at the Hyde Park State Bank. And with the letters sent to Morton D. Ballard at the Morrison, as with also his checkbook, not checkbook, his bank book from the Hyde Park State Bank. He told the Rent-A-Car people that he was a salesman new on the route. That was the first time he had covered this district. He was a salesman from Peoria, and that the only person he knew in Chicago was a Mr. Louis Mason.

He told them this because the Rent-A-Car people demand three in-town references in order to take out a car. However, he wanted to persuade them to give him the car. Anyhow, in view of the fact that he was new, and that Mr. Louis Mason would vouch for him, and also because he would be willing to deposit $400 there if necessary, in order to get the car. I was posted in a little restaurant or cigar store on Wabash Avenue. Do you want the exact name?

Q. Yes, if you recall the address?

A. This cigar store is a little bit north of

16th Street, on the west side of Wabash Avenue. I went in this cigar store and sat near the public phone booth, whose number Leopold had, and he told them this number was the number of Mr. Louis Mason. The Rent-A-Car people called up, and I immediately answered the phone and told them I was Mr. Mason.

Q. You are in this cigar store, now, or in the vicinity of 16th Street, near the Rent-A-Car people?

A. Yes.

Q. And you placed yourself at the booth?

A. Yes. The phone rang, and I immediately answered the phone, and the Rent-A-Car people asked me if I was Mr. Louis Mason. I said yes. They asked me if I knew Mr. Morton D. Ballard of Peoria. I said, "Yes." They asked me if he was dependable. I said, "Absolutely dependable." That was the end of the conversation.

Q. You were posing as Mr. Ballard?

A. No, I was posing as Mr. Louis Mason. Leopold succeeded in getting the car and told the Rent-A-Car people to forward the identification card, which they demand as necessary to get a car anytime without the trouble of getting references over again, and everything he asked them to forward this identification card to the Morrison Hotel.

We took the car out that morning at eleven and returned it at four. Then we went down to the Morrison Hotel, and I went inside to check out. I went up to the room and found the suitcase had disappeared from the room.

Q. You have references to the suitcase which you had taken there when you registered?

A. Yes. I realized then that the maid must have gotten suspicious due to the fact that the bed had not been slept in either night. And with her suspicions aroused, that she had opened the suitcase and found only those books in the suitcase. Therefore, I immediately left the room and left the hotel. We phoned the Rent-A-Car people and told them to forward the identification card to the Trenier Hotel.

Q. That is located where?

A. At the corner of Oakwood Boulevard and Grand.

Q. Did any mail come forth from the conversation?
A. No. In order to assume some sort of identity there, Leopold went in and told them that he was Morton D. Ballard, that he had intended stopping at the Trenier, but that he was not going to, and that if any letters came for him there, they should hold them there at the Trenier Hotel.
We mailed two letters to the Trenier Hotel, to Mr. Morton D. Ballard, at the Trenier hotel, in order that the clerk would think that there was someone expecting mail there so that when the card came from the Rent-A-Car people, it would be safe. However, neither the card from the Rent-A-Car people nor, curiously enough, our own letters, which we know we had mailed to the Trenier Hotel, arrived there.
Q. Now, on the 21st day of May 1924, just tell where you met Leopold and what happened. State it in your own words.
A. On the 21st of May, I met Leopold out of school at eleven o'clock. Wait a minute. Perhaps I better start with the 20th of May.

Q. Very well.
A. On the 20th of May, Leopold and I purchased at two hardware stores on Cottage Grove Avenue some rope...
Q. In what vicinity was that?
A. Cottage Grove Avenue. Both of the hardware stores, I believe, although I am not certain, were somewhere out there shortly north of 43rd Street. The hardware store where we purchased the rope was further north than the hardware store where we purchased the chisel. I purchased myself, alone, both the chisel and rope. We then proceeded down the street to a drug store, where Leopold tried to purchase hydrochloric acid. He was unsuccessful at that drug store, so he went a little bit further south. I don't know the exact number where he succeeded in purchasing a bottle of hydrochloric acid.
Q. Where did you get the gags?
A. The gags were at Leopold's house.
Q. You didn't get them on the same day that you purchased the chisel and the hydrochloric acid and rope, did you?
A. We got them ready at his house.

Q. All right. After purchasing these different articles, what did you do?
A. We proceeded to his house, where we got everything in readiness, some ether that he had at his house, the ropes, and the rags to be used as gags, the chisel which he bound with adhesive tape on the sharp end, some hip boots that I believe belonged to his brother…
Q. Where did you get those hip boots?
A. I believe they belonged to his brother. They were at his house.
Q. This is all, now, with reference to the 20th day?
A. Yes. Everything was gotten in readiness. I believe also on that day the various notes and telephone messages, pardon me, the various notes were written on the typewriter for Mr. Franks.
Q. Did you see him write any notes on the typewriter?
A. Yes, I saw him write all of them.
Q. What notes do you have reference to?
A. I have reference to the note demanding the $10,000 in ransom.
Q. What kind of a typewriter was that?
A. An Underwood portable typewriter.
Q. On a portable Underwood

typewriter?
A. Yes.
Q. And what was the essence of that note?
A. The essence of that note demanded $10,000. And it told Mr. Franks that his son was safe, specified a certain way in which the money should be wrapped in a cigar box, and told Mr. Franks that everything would be all right, the son would be returned to him within six hours if he obeyed our instructions. But that if he disobeyed any of the instructions, that his son would be killed.
Q. Now, who composed that note?
A. The note was composed jointly.
Q. And it was typed by Leopold?
A. Yes.
Q. Do you recall the words used in that note? To the best of your recollection, what were they?
A. "Dear Sir, you no doubt know by this time that your son has been kidnapped. Please follow our instructions carefully and nothing will happen to him. If you don't follow our instructions to the letter, you will never see your son again." Then there was a number one, and "Go down

to the bank and get ten thousand." No, that wasn't it, wait a minute. The number one was, "Do not communicate with the police. If you have already done so, please do not mention this letter." Number 2, "Go down to the bank and get $10,000. In old bills. Be sure that the bills are old."

Q. Did you specify any denominations?

A. Yes. Any new or marked bills will be noticed. "Get $2,000. In twenty-dollar bills and $8,000. In fifty-dollar bills." Number three, "Be home by one o'clock. Do not let the phone be used."

Q. Is that all?

A. There was at the end, I don't remember.

Q. Do you recall any other note that was written that day?

A. I think the other two notes were written on that same day. All the notes and telephone messages had been written in rough draft some days before that. So, all that was done on Tuesday, as I remember, was to copy those things. I dictated while Leopold typewrote. Proceeding to the 21st, I met Leopold at school at eleven. We…

Q. That is on the 21st day?
A. Yes. We went downtown…
Q. In whose car?
A. In his Willys-Knight, parking the car on 16th Street just east of Michigan Boulevard, on the south side of the street. Leopold went to the Rent-A-Car people again, carrying his letters, supposedly to Morton D. Ballard and sufficient money.
Q. The purpose of the letters was to show he was identified?
A. Yes. He told the Rent-A-Car people that he had not received the identification card but that he would like to take out the car. They offered no objection, so after a short time, he received his car, which was a Willys-Knight five-passenger touring car, blue in color, with no further identification marks. In other words, there were no windshields. In other words, the car was equipped with only standard equipment. He passed by me down 16th Street, no pardon me, I saw him coming in the car, and as prearranged, jumped into his car and went to Kramer's Restaurant at the corner of 35th and Cottage.

Q. And what did you do with Leopold's car?
A. We parked both cars at Kramer's and proceeded to put up the side curtains on the Willys-Knight.
Q. That you had rented from the Rent-A-Car people?
A. Yes. We ate lunch at Kramer's and left Kramer's...
Q. About what time was it when you left Kramer's?
A. About one.
Q. And you left in whose car?
A. We left with both cars.
Q. And the curtains up on the Willys-Knight that you had gotten from the Rent-A-Car people?
A. Yes.
Q. And where did you go from there?
A. We parked Leopold's car at his garage, which is situated in the back of his house. I was driving the Rent-A-Car Willys. He joined me immediately after having disposed of his car. We went out to Jackson Park, where we parked for, I should judge, between three-quarters of an hour to an hour because we wanted to

wait until the Harvard School let out before starting any operations.

At about 2:15, we left Jackson Park and drove in the Willys to Ingleside Avenue, where we parked just south of an alley on the east side of the street.

Q. Did you have at that time in this car in which you were riding and which you parked down by the alley around Ingleside, the hydrochloric acid and the boots, rope, and chisel?

A. Yes, sir. We had all that. I think now that I come to think of it, that when he went to the garage to dispose of his car, I followed him in the other Willys, and we changed the contents of his car.

Q. Meaning the hydrochloric acid, the boots, rope, gag, and chisel?

A. Yes, to the Rent-A-Car people car.

Q. Now, you are down there on Ingleside Avenue waiting for the kids to come out of the Harvard School?

A. Yes. I walked over to the Harvard School to reconnoiter.

Q. And that is about what time?

A. Just about two-twenty.

Q. You are over there for the purpose of reconnoitering?

A. Yes, sir.
Q. Go ahead.
A. I talked to a fellow by the name of Cease.
Q. Who is this man Cease?
A. He is the tutor who takes out the children.
Q. After classes?
A. In the afternoon, to supervise their play. I talked to him for a few moments and then talked to a young boy by the name of...
Q. What did you talk to Cease about?
A. I don't remember.
Q. Then you talked with whom else?
A. With a little boy by the name of Levinson, John Levinson, whom I knew. I just asked Levinson about his baseball game, and so forth, and so on.
I left Harvard School, then that is, I left. Pardon me, I left the back of the playground where I had been talking to Cease and Levinson and went out in front of the Harvard School, where I met my little brother, who attends that school. I talked to him for a short time, and then Leopold came down Ellis Avenue on the west side of the street and whistled for

me to come over. He walked down the alley leading to Ingleside, the same alley near which the car was parked, and told me that there were some children playing on Ingleside Avenue that he thought may be possible prospects.

Q. For kidnapping?

A. For kidnapping, yes. We decided, however, not to get them and walked down Drexel Boulevard to where we saw a group of children playing on a vacant lot at the southeast corner of Drexel and 49th Street. We watched these boys and noticed that Levinson was amongst them.

Q. What was his first name? John Levinson?

A. I think so. We went back to the car, got the car, and drove to the west side of Drexel, opposite to where the children were playing. We looked to see if we could recognize them from a distance, but it was very difficult, so we walked down to 50th Street and around 50th Street through an alley where we could watch them more closely. Even from there, however, it was impossible to watch them very closely unless we showed ourselves, so we decided to go

back to his car, drive over to his house and get a pair of bird glasses.
Q. You mean field glasses?
A. Well, yes, field glasses, and watch the children through the field glasses. This we did. While he was getting the field glasses, I went to a drug store on the corner of 47th and Ellis, where I looked up the address of Mr. Levinson so that we would be able to tell where John lived. I incidentally bought a couple of packages of Dentyne chewing gum at the drug store.
I picked Leopold up immediately after that with the field glasses, and we went over to the same place on Drexel Boulevard. We watched the children some more through the field glasses and noted that Levinson, with a group of some of the other children, went down the alleyway out of sight. We didn't think that he had gone home, so we remained watching. But when after quite a while he didn't show up, we came to the conclusion that he might have gone home.
I went to look for him in the alley but didn't see him and saw Cease leaving

with the rest of his children. We then went to a corner lot at the corner of 48th and Greenwood, the northeast corner, where John Coleman and Walter Baer's sons were playing baseball. We watched them for a little while, then went down to see if Levinson had gone home, passed his house, and found that he was not there or playing on the street. We returned down Lake Park Avenue, passed the lot where the Coleman boy was playing and went into Leopold's house to watch the children play from one of the windows there. We didn't stay there long but left and drove down Drexel to go past this lot where Levinson had been playing, turned, and went down Hyde Park Boulevard, turned and went north on Ellis Avenue.

All this time, I was driving. We proceeded north on Ellis Avenue until we caught a glimpse of Robert Franks coming south on the west side of Ellis Avenue. As we passed him, he was just coming across or past 48th Street. We turned down 48th Street and turned the car around. Leopold got into the back seat. I drove the car, then, south on Ellis Avenue, parallel to where young Franks was, stopped the car, and while remaining in my seat, opened the front door and called to Franks that I would give him a ride home. He said no. He would just as soon walk, but I told him that I would like to talk to him about a tennis racket, so he got in the car.

We proceeded south on Ellis Avenue, turned east on 50th Street, and just after we turned off Ellis Avenue, Leopold reached his arm around young Franks, grabbed his mouth, and hit him over the head with the chisel. I believe he hit him several times. I do not know the exact number. He began to bleed and was not entirely unconscious. He was moaning. I proceeded further east on 50th and turned, I believe, at Dorchester. At this point, Leopold...

Q. What time was it?

A. This was around five o'clock. I don't know the exact time. At this time, Leopold grabbed Franks and carried him over back of the front seat, and threw him on a rug in the car. He then took one of the rags and gagged him by sticking it down his throat, I believe. We proceeded down Dorchester, and then at Leopold's direction, drove into the country.

I think we drove either out Jeffery Road or South Shore Drive. I think it was Jeffery Road. I am not acquainted with the district out there and drove slowly at his directions. Plus, the fact of my excitement accounts for my not being able to tell any of the places we drove. However, we drove until we were at a deserted road which led off the main road somewhere before the Indiana line. We turned down this road, but it was only for, it was only a road for a short distance, and ended in a blank. This Leopold knew but wanted to take it because it was deserted.

We turned around and as we turned around, he, seeing that Franks was unconscious, climbed into the front seat. Up to that time, he had been watching him from the back seat. He had covered him up with the robe that we had brought along, the robe also belonging to Leopold. We then drove further south on the main highway until we turned at a road, which I believe leads to Gary. We went down this road a ways and then turned off the road on another deserted road. This deserted road was leading north.

We followed that for only a short distance, then turned down another deserted road leading west. We stopped the car, got out, removed young Franks' shoes, hid them in some bushes, and removed his pants and stockings, placing them in the car. We did this in order that we might be saved the trouble of too much undressing him later on. We also left his belt buckle and belt with the shoes, not in the same place, but very nearby. We proceeded to drive around back and forth and forth and back.

Q. Waiting for it to get dark?

A. Waiting for it to get dark. We stopped at a little sandwich shop on the road, and Leopold got out and purchased a couple of red-hot sandwiches and two bottles of root beer. We then kept driving more and more until it was fairly dusk.

Then Leopold wanted to make a phone call. The phone call had nothing to do with the Franks case. He made this phone call from a drug store situated on the northeast corner of one of the intersecting streets meeting this main highway, the name of which I do not know. The important thing is that I parked the car on this side of the street, facing west, parallel to the tracks. The driver's seat is on the left of the car. Therefore, I was nearest to the drugstore. He got out of the car, went to the drug store, and made his phone call. In returning, he came straight to the car, so that he hit the door that I was sitting at, rather than the door next to the vacant seat, and he said, "Slip over and let me drive for a while," which I did.

He drove the car. We again proceeded down the thoroughfare, waiting for it to get dark. I remember we turned up one road which he said led to Indianapolis and back again, and finally, he drove the car to a place where he knew was near this culvert. We had both investigated the culvert on a previous journey out there some weeks before.

Q. When you had planned it, you mean?
A. Yes. We dragged the body out of the car, put the body in the robe, and carried it over to the culvert. Leopold carried the

feet, and I carried the head. We deposited the body near the culvert and undressed the body completely. Our original scheme had been to etherize the boy to death.

Q. Where did you pour the hydrochloric acid on him?

A. Right there. The scheme for etherizing him originated through Leopold, who eventually has some knowledge of such things, and he said that that would be the easiest way of putting him to death and the least messy. This, however, we found unnecessary because the boy was quite dead when we took him there. We knew he was dead, by the fact that rigor mortis had set in, and also by his eyes, and then when at that same time we poured this hydrochloric acid over him, we noticed no tremor, not a single tremor in his body, therefore, we were sure he was dead.

Leopold put on his hip boots, taking off his coat in order to do this, and took the body and stuck it headfirst…

Captain William Shoemacher: Q. Was it dark at that time?

A. Yes, stuck it headfirst into the culvert.

I might say that at this time, it was fairly dark but still not pitch black so that we were able to work without a flashlight.
Assistant State Attorney John Sbarbaro:
Q. How far did you have to carry the body, from the time you got off the machine until you dropped it down into or near the culvert?
A. I should say about a city block and a half. I don't know.
Q. How did you carry it? In this blanket?
A. In the blanket, yes. That is, we had the blanket, in sort of, as you might use a stretcher.
Q. Well, then, you put the body right down into the culvert?
A. Yes.
Q. And you poured your hydrochloric acid on it?
A. Before we put it down in the culvert.
Q. And then what did you do?
A. Then I went to the opposite side of the culvert, where the water runs out, and where you can get at the water very easily, where I washed my hands which had become bloody through carrying the body.
Q. The head had bled very freely?

A. Yes, the head had bled quite freely, I wouldn't say very freely, but quite freely. There was quite a bit of blood. The blanket or robe was quite saturated with blood. We then left, taking the robe we used, as also the clothing of young Franks, and we started homeward. Leopold stopped to call up his folks to tell them that he would be slightly detained. This, I should judge, was about nine o'clock. We then stopped at a drug store somewhere in the neighborhood, where I looked up the address of Jacob Franks and the telephone number, and at the same time, Leopold printed the address on the envelope. We then proceeded toward home.

Q. You drove out to Gary, didn't you before you go to the culvert?
A. No, I don't think we ever entered Gary.
Q. Well, near Gary?
A. Well, near Gary.
Q. But it was near Gary, though, when you stripped the kid of the shoes?
A. Yes.
Q. And his pants and stockings?
A. Yes.

Q. In what vicinity were you in when Leopold made this first phone call?
A. I think that we were in the town of Hammond. The road we were on led north and south; I am practically positive.
Q. Did you make the change at the wheel there?
A. That is where we alternated the drive.
Q. And what did you do at that end of the machine?
A. Do you want me to go on with this?
Q. Yes, finish what you started.
A. I am not sure whether we posted the letter before or after destroying Franks' clothing. However, what we did do was to go over to my house, where we burned the clothing in the furnace.
Q. Did you burn the blanket too, in which you had the clothing wrapped?
A. No, the blanket was placed in a little hiding place near the greenhouse at my house. After having burned the clothing, we proceeded to get a pail, soap, and brush, and to the best of our ability, in the dark, to try and wash out the car of bloodstains. The car at this time, when we were washing out the bloodstains, was

THE CONFESSION OF RICHARD LOEB | 89

parked on 50th Street, near the greenhouse. I think that we probably mailed the letter, the ransom letter, to Mr. Franks before we burned the clothing. No, I don't know, at that.
Captain William Shoemacher: Q. Where was it mailed at?
A. The letter was mailed right opposite from the Hyde Park post office, and I think it was mailed. In fact, I am quite sure it was mailed before the clothing was destroyed.
Q. When would that be, about?
A. That would be about ten o'clock, or a quarter to ten, at the Hyde Park station. Immediately after having destroyed the clothes, washed the car, and hid the blanket, we proceeded to a drug store on the northeast corner of either Greenwood or Woodlawn on 47th Street, where Leopold phoned Mrs. Franks, telling her that her son had been kidnapped.
We then parked the car just north of where Leopold lives on Greenwood Avenue, on the west side of the street, and entered the Leopold home. Leopold took home his aunt and uncle, Mr. and

Mrs. Schwab. I sat with Mr. Leopold for a while until Leopold came back. Then we drank a while, played cards, and then we left. He took me home in his own car, which he had taken from the garage in order to take his aunt and uncle home.
Q. What time was it, about then?
A. About ten-thirty, I should judge. On the way home, we threw the chisel out of the car on Greenwood Avenue, someplace between 48th and 50th. He took me home. The next morning, he came over to my house around eleven-thirty.

Assistant State Attorney John Sbarbaro:
Q. Was that the day that you disposed of the other articles, like the Underwood?
A. No, this was the next day after the crime. The next day Leopold came over to my house at about eleven-thirty, and I dressed and selected a black overcoat and hat of my father's to wear for the afternoon. I left them home and went out with Leopold, dressed as I usually do. We went to the Cooper-Carlton for lunch, where we had lunch with Richard Rubel, the three of us together.

Immediately after lunch, we went over to

my house. I changed my overcoat and cap for the black overcoat and cap or hat of my father's. We went over to Leopold's, and there I changed overcoats again, selecting an overcoat that was less conspicuous that happened to be lying around the hallway there. We then took the rented car, the Willys-Knight, which had been parked all night at the same place, and drove it around to the garage, where we attempted to wash out the bloodstains with soap and water.
Q. Was that Leopold's garage?
A. Yes. Leopold's chauffeur came out, and we told him that we were washing out marks of wine from the car.
Q. You had reference to the red bloodstains, then, didn't you?
A. Yes. Upon leaving Leopold's, we proceed downtown in both the Willys-Knights, I driving the rented car, Willys-Knight. We stopped at the corner of the Oakwood and Vincennes. We, both of us, got out of the car and went to the corner of Pershing Road and Vincennes, where there is a "Keep the City Clean" box.
We left a note in this "Keep the City

Clean" box, reading to this effect: That Mr. Franks was to come, was to go immediately to the Bogert de Ross or something drug store at the corner of 63rd and Blackstone, and wait there in a specified phone booth for a phone call. However, the letter did not stick to the "Keep the City Clean" box with the stickers we had provided for it. Fearing that it might blow away, or somebody might open the box and have it blow away, we decided that the best thing to do was to entirely omit this letter from our calculations. And when we phoned Mr. Franks, instead of telling him to go to the "Keep the city clean" box where he would receive a note telling him what to do further, to phone his house, telling him to immediately go to the Bogert de Ross drug store on 63rd Street.

After having placed the letter in the "Keep the city clean" box, we proceeded downtown in both cars. We parked Leopold's Willys-Knight on Wabash Avenue near 16th Street and proceeded to the Illinois Central Station in the Rent-A-Car Willys-Knight. We stopped there, and I went out and purchased a ticket to Michigan City and a berth, wearing glasses, in order to disguise myself, as also the black hat and overcoat.

At two-thirty, the three o'clock train which runs on the Michigan Central as far as Boston is made up. Therefore, at two-thirty, I went down the train, got on the train, and left a note, which we had prepared in the box provided for telegraph blanks.

This note instructed Mr. Franks to go immediately to the back platform of the train, to watch the east side of the track, and to wait until he had entirely passed the first large red brick factory with a water tower on top of it. The factory had the word "Champion" written on the water tower. After he had completely passed this water tower or this factory, he was to count to five quickly and throw the package as far east as he could.

At the same time, while I was placing the letter on the train, Leopold was phoning the Yellow Cab Company to send a cab to Franks and also telling Franks to go to the Bogert de Ross drug store. We jumped in our car immediately. It was then about two-thirty-three. We drove quickly to 67th Street and Stony Island, parking the car on the southwest corner of 67th and Stony Island. We got out of the car and noticed a newsstand that was there, where papers were on sale, showing that an unidentified nude boy had been found out around 121st and Railroad Avenue at the Pennsylvania tracks. We had intended phoning Mr. Franks from the Walgreen drug store at the southeast corner of 67th and Stony Island. We had intended phoning him to the Bogert de Ross drug store, telling him to get on this train, to purchase a ticket to Michigan City, and to look in car 507 for the communication which would tell him or which would give him further instructions.

We debated then what we should do, in view of the boy's body having been discovered. I was not very anxious to go on with the matter, but Leopold persuaded me to go ahead with the thing. So, he phoned Mr. Franks at the Bogert de Ross drug store, and finding out that Mr. Franks was not there, we went to another drug store further south on

THE CONFESSION OF RICHARD LOEB | 95

Stony Island, where he again phoned the Bogert de Ross drug store, again finding out that Mr. Franks was not there.
We then realized that the body had been identified a that of Robert Franks and that any further attempt to get the money would only result in failure. We, therefore, immediately went downtown to the Rent-A-Car place, and Leopold took in the car. I stayed outside, in the Willys-Knight, in the red Willys, which had been parked there.
I then returned home, got home about five, and was told of the Franks murder by the chauffeur, who showed me one of the newspapers. Nothing else transpired of importance until Saturday night. Late Saturday night, around two o'clock, I met Leopold at a restaurant next to the garage, the Fashion Garage at the corner of 51st and Cottage. He had this car, and we took his car in which he had placed his typewriter, the Underwood portable typewriter, upon which the letters had been written. And we took the typewriter out of the back trunk, brought it into the front seat, and I took a pair of pliers and pried off the keys, just the very tips of

the keys, where the imprints would show. We took these keys in a little bundle and threw them off the bridge in Jackson Park, situated near the golden Statute of Liberty. Then we took the typewriter, intact with the case, and threw it off the bridge leading to the outer harbor. In other words, the bridge. The big tone bridge with the pyramid effects at all four corners of the bridge. It is the bridge leading to the outer harbor. The typewriter was thrown on the east side of the bridge.

The robe was then taken from its hiding place. We went over to Leopold's garage and got some gasoline, took the robe out on South Shore Drive, on a little side street connecting with South Shore Drive, and saturated the robe with gasoline, and set fire to it. That is all I have to tell you about the murder of Robert Franks.

Q. And this statement that you have just made has been made of your own free will?

A. Yes. I just want to say that I offer no excuse but that I am fully convinced that neither the idea nor the act would have occurred to me had it not been for the suggestion and stimulus of Leopold. Furthermore, I do not believe that I would have been capable of having killed Franks. This statement is made of my own volition.

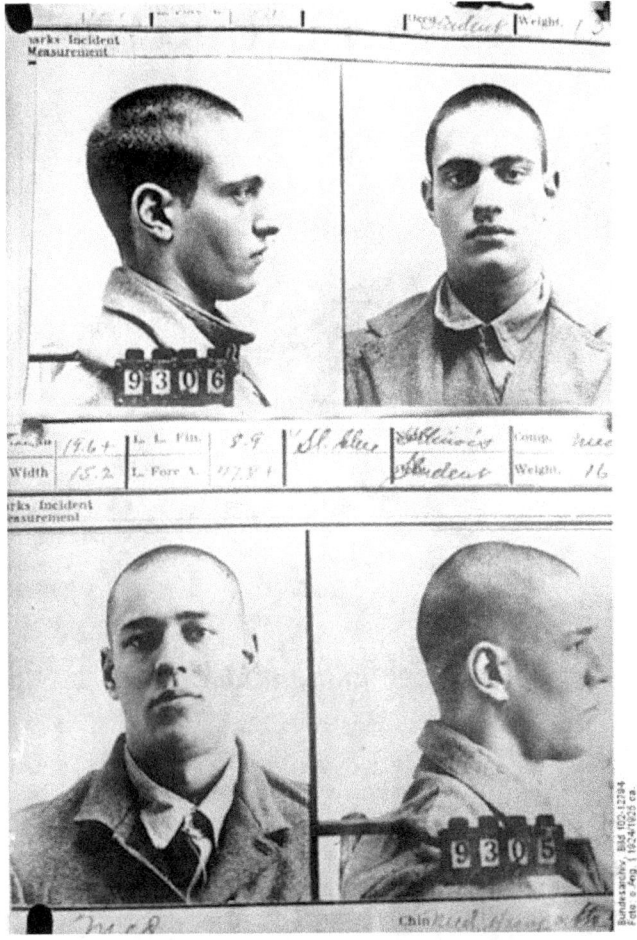

Leopold (top) & Loeb (bottom) mug shots

4

THE CONFESSION OF NATHAN LEOPOLD

Car used in the abduction

On May 31, 1924, Nathan Leopold Jr. also made his confession to the kidnapping and murder of Robert Franks at 4:20 a.m. The questions were asked by Assistant State Attorney

Joseph P. Savage and Chief of Detectives Michael Hughes at the office of the State's Attorney of Cook County, Chicago, Illinois.

Assistant State Attorney Joseph P. Savage: Q. What is your name?
Nathan Leopold: A. Nathan F. Leopold Junior.
Q. And you address?
A. 4754 Greenwood Avenue.
Q. And your business?
A. Student.
Q. Student at what school?
A. University of Chicago Law School.
Q. And you have attended the University of Chicago Law School for how long?
A. For nine months.
Q. Prior to that time, what school did you attend?
A. University of Chicago.
Q. And for how long during that period?
A. For a year.
Q. And prior to that?
A. University of Michigan for a year. Prior to that, the University of Chicago for a year. Prior to that, Harvard School

for five years. Prior to that, Douglas School for four years. Prior to that, Spade School for two years.
Q. How old are you, Nathan?
A. Nineteen.
Q. What is the date of your birth?
A. November 19, 1904.
Q. Have you any brothers, Nathan?
A. I have two brothers.
Q. What are their names?
A. Foreman and Samuel Leopold.
Q. And you have one other?
A. A cousin who lives with us, Adolf Ballenberger.
Q. Your father's name?
A. Nathan F. Leopold.
Q. What is his business?
A. Morris Paper Mills.
Q. Now, Nathan, I just want you to go on in your own way and tell us the story from the beginning. Tell us the whole thing.
A. When we planned a general thing of this sort, it was as long ago as last November, I guess as least, and we started on the process of how to get the money, which was much the most difficult problem. We had, oh, several

dozen different plans, all of which were not good, for one reason or another. Finally, hit upon the plan of having the money thrown from a moving train after the train had passed a given landmark. The landmark we finally chose was the factory of the champion Manufacturing Company at 74th Street and the I.C. Railroad tracks.

The next problem was the system of notification to the father. We originally planned a number of relays. In other words, the man was to receive a special delivery letter telling him that his son had been kidnapped and was being held for ransom. Then, to secure ten thousand dollars in denominations as follows: eight thousand dollars in fifty-dollar bills, two thousand dollars in twenty-dollar bills. He was to get old, unmarked bills whose numbers were not in sequence, and these he was to place in a cigar box, securely tied, wrapped in white paper, the ends were to be sealed with sealing wax. The reason for this was to give the impression that the box would be delivered personally to a messenger of the real executives of the plan.

He was then to receive a phone call at about one or two o'clock in the afternoon, instructing him to proceed to a '"Help Keep the City Clean" box, whose location was to be definitely given. Then, he was to find another note which would instruct him to proceed to a drugstore that had a public phone booth. He was to be called at this phone booth, the drugstore being very near the I.C. track, and given only just enough time to rush out, buy a ticket and board a through train without allowing him enough to instruct detectives or police where he was going.

In the train, he was to proceed to the rear car and look in the box left for telegraph blanks for another letter. This letter instructed him to go to the rear platform of the car, face east and look for the first large red brick factory adjacent to the tracks, which had a black water tower bearing a white inscription, "Champion." He was to count two or three after that and throw the box as far to the east as he could.

The next problem was getting the victim to kill. This was left undecided until the day we decided to take the most likely looking subject that came our way. The particular occasion happened to be Robert Franks. Richard was acquainted with Robert and asked him to come over to our car for a moment. This occurred near 49th and Ellis Avenue. Robert came over to the car, was introduced to me, and Richard asked him if he wanted a ride home.

Q. Richard, who?

A. Richard Loeb. He replied no, but Richard said, "Well, get in a minute. I want to ask you about a certain tennis racket." After he had gotten in, I stepped on the gas, proceeded south on Ellis Avenue to 50th Street. In the meantime, Richard asked Robert if he minded if we took him around the block, to which Robert said, "No."

As soon as we turned the corner, Richard placed his one hand over Robert's mouth to stifle his outcries, and with his right, beat him on the head several times with a chisel, specially prepared for the purpose. The boy did not succumb as readily as we had believed, so for fear of being observed, Richard seized him, pulled him into the back seat. Here, he forced a cloth into his mouth. Apparently, the boy died instantly by suffocation shortly thereafter.

We proceeded out to Calumet Boulevard in Indiana, drove along this road that leads to Gary, being a rather deserted place. We even stopped to buy a couple of sandwiches for supper.

Q. Where?

A. On Calumet Boulevard at, I guess, 132nd Street. The body was covered by an automobile robe which had been brought along for the purpose. We drove around up and down this road, then proceeded over the path which leads out toward Hegewisch, from 108th and Avenue F to the prearranged spot for the disposal of the body.

We had previously removed the shoes, socks, and trousers of the boy, leaving the shoes and the belt by the side of the road, concealed in the grass. Having arrived at our destination, we placed the body in the robe, carried it to the culvert where it was found. Here we completed the disrobing, then in an attempt to render identification more difficult, poured hydrochloric acid over the face and body. Then, we placed the body into the drainpipe and pushed it in as far as we could. We gathered up all the clothes and placed them in the robe.

Apparently, at this point, the glasses fell from my pocket. I carried the robe containing the clothes back to the automobile, a distance of some 300 yards, and one of the socks apparently dropped from the bundle. We then proceeded north to 104th and Ewing Avenue, from where I telephoned my folks, telling them that I should be a trifle late in arriving home.

We then drove to 47th and Woodlawn, and from there, I telephoned the Franks' home. I spo
ke to Mrs. Franks and told her that my name was George Johnson and that her boy had been kidnapped but was safe and the further instructions would follow. In passing 55th Street, we had mailed the special delivery letter, which had been completed except for the address which I printed on. After taking my aunt and uncle home, I returned to my home. And after my father had retired, Richard and

I proceeded to his home, where we burned the remaining clothes, hid the robe, and washed the more obvious bloodstains from the automobile.

Then I parked the automobile near my home. The next day at two-thirty Central time, or three-thirty Chicago time, we were down at the Illinois Central station at 12th Street. Here, Richard bought a ticket to Michigan City on the three o'clock train, entered the train, and deposited the letter in the telegraph blank box.

In the meantime, I called the Franks' home, told Mr. Franks to proceed immediately to a drugstore at 1465 East 63rd Street and to wait at the more easterly of the two public phone booths for a telephone call. I told him a Yellow Cab would be at his door to take him. I repeated the number twice, and he asked if he couldn't have a little more time, to which I replied no, it must be immediate. About the time I was finished, Richard had returned from the train, and he started out south intending to call the drugstore from Walgreen's drugstore at 67th and Stony Island. We chanced to see a newspaper lying on the stand with headlines, "Unidentified Boy Found in Swamp." We deliberated a few moments as to what to do, Dick thinking that the game was up. I, however, insisted that it could do no harm to call the drugstore. This I did but was told that Mr. Franks was in the building.

We then went to 60th and Stoney Island, another drugstore, and again telephoned. We met with the same reply. Then we gave it up as a bad job and returned the car to the place where it had been rented. Our original plan had included a relay which was to send Mr. Franks to a "Help Keep the City Clean" box at the corner of Vincennes at Pershing, but we had difficulty in making the envelope stick to the cover of the box as we intended, and hence decided to eliminate this relay.

Thursday, immediately after dinner, we drove the car to our garage and started to clean up the rest of the bloodstains. Our chauffeur, Sven Englund, noticed us and came out to help. Whereupon Richard told him it was merely some red wine which had been spilled.

Q. Who did the clean-up?
A. Dick did most of it, and I helped him.
Q. Is anything else you can think of at this time?
A. No.
Q. Your original plan when you were thinking it out as late as last November, now, then, did you have in mind at that time who was to be the victim?
A. Nobody, in particular. We had considered Mr. Clarence Coleman; also Mr. Walter Baer, Walter Baer Jr., as the victim and Clarence Coleman's son.
Q. When was the plan finally effected whereby you considered the Franks boy?
A. When we saw him on the street, by pure accident.
Q. At that time, were you waiting for someone else?
A. We had been cruising around, watching several groups of boys playing, waiting for somebody to start home.
Q. You had been doing that for how long, Nathan?
A. From about three o'clock in the afternoon until about five.
Q. And you didn't have any boys prior to that time?

A. No.

Q. This day, in particular, you set out with the idea in mind of getting a boy that day, is that it?

A. Yes, sir.

Q. What time did you meet Richard Loeb that day, Wednesday, May 21, 1924?

A. At eleven o'clock.

Q. Where did you meet him?

A. At the University.

Q. What did you do after that?

A. Drove down in my car to the Rent-A-Car place.

Q. Where is that at?

A. That is at 1408 or '10 Michigan Avenue.

Q. Then what did you do?

A. Rented a Willys-Knight.

Q. At that time?

A. Yes.

Q. Under what name?

A. Morton D. Ballard.

Q. Had you ever rented a car there before?

A. Yes, sir.

Q. Under what name?

A. The same.

Q. When did you rent a car there?
A. About three weeks previous.
Q. And used it for what purpose?
A. Merely so we would have no difficulty in getting the car the next time.
Q. They handle Willys-Knights and Fords?
A. Willys-Knights and Fords.
Q. Willys-Knights and Fords exclusively, is that right?
A. Yes.
Q. What did you pay over there?
A. 17 cents a mile for Willys, and 15 cents a mile for Fords.
Q. You could keep the car overnight?
A. Yes, we made that arrangement Wednesday.
Q. After you got the car, what time did you get the car down there that day?
A. At eleven-thirty.
Q. Do you remember who talked to you there, Nathan?
A. It was one of two men, I don't remember.
Q. Can you remember the names?
A. No.
Q. You would know them if you would see them?

A. Yes.

Q. If I came over there for a car, would they require any security?

A. Yes, the first time they made me deposit fifty dollars, and the last time thirty-five. I was supposed to have an identification card of some sort, but I never received it, so I had to look up my old lease number and give that as a reference.

Q. What address did you give, Nathan?

A. Originally, the Morrison Hotel. We went down there and rented a room, left a suitcase in it, and sent some mail there, for the purpose of having mail addressed to that address. When we went down there to get our mail on a subsequent date, the suitcase had been taken. Apparently, the fact that the beds had not been used had been noticed, and some suspicion occurred. The suitcase apparently had been confiscated. I, therefore, telephoned the Rent-A-Car place and told them that we had changed our hotel to Oakwood and Grand.

Q. You phoned there immediately that was your new address?

A. Yes, sir.

Q. Did you ever get your suitcase, Nathan, from the Morrison Hotel?
A. No.
Q. Did you register at the Morrison Hotel?
A. I didn't. Richard did.
Q Under the name of?
A. Morrison D. Ballard.
Q. What day was that? Do you remember, Nathan?
A. That was just previously to our getting the first car, I would say two or three weeks before.
Q. Whose suitcase was it?
A. Dick's.
Q. You never applied for the suitcase after that?
A. No, I figured the suitcase was worth less than what we owed.
Q. What kind of suitcase was it?
A. It was a dilapidated suitcase. I could not describe it very well.
Q. Do you remember anything in it?
A. I think there were some library books in it.
Q. You went then to this, what is the name of that hotel?
A. The Trenier Hotel. I had expected to

stop there but had changed my plans and asked them to hold mail coming for Morton D. Ballard. I stopped there on a number of occasions after that. I would say as much as half a dozen times and never did get any mail from there. This seems very peculiar, inasmuch as Richard addressed two letters to the Trenier hotel, and they were never received.
Q. Did you get the letters back?
A. No. No return address on them.
Q. Went in the dead letter office?
A. I don't see why they should have. We followed them up two days afterward.
Q. You say you did stop there several times after that?
A. Yes, a number of times.
Chief Detective Michael Hughes: Q. You stopped there to call for the mail?
A. Yes.
Q. You did not register there?
A. No.
Assistant State Attorney Joseph P. Savage: Q. At no time registered there?
A. No.
Q. Did you ever register in any other hotel, Nathan, during this period?
A. No. I further opened a bank balance

in the Hyde Part State bank, corner of 53rd and Lake Park.
Q. Under the name of Morton D. Ballard?
A. Yes.
Q. How much money did you deposit there?
A. One hundred dollars.
Q. Have you drawn that out since that time?
A. Yes.
Q. Was it a checking account?
A. Checking account.
Q. And you have a balance in the bank now?
A. No, sir.
Q. That was opened up there during your negotiations with the people on Michigan Avenue?
A. Yes, sir.
Q. What was that name, again?
A. Rent-A-Car.
Q. That was for the purpose of?
A. Having a good identification.
Q. This day you went down there for the car, who drove the cat out?
A. I did.
Q. Where was your car at that time?

A. Dick had my car on 14th Street, just east of Michigan Boulevard.
Q. When you left there, what did you do?
A. We drove up together, or rather, we each drove one car up to Kramer's restaurant, 35th and Cottage?
Q. Kramer's restaurant, 35th and Cottage?
A. Yes.
Q. That was on Wednesday, the 21st?
A. Wednesday, the 21st.
Q. 1924?
A. 1924.
Q. May 21st, 1924?
A. Yes.
Q. Kramer's Restaurant was where?
A. 35th and Cottage Grove Avenue.
Q. What did you do?
A. Had lunch there.
Q. You had lunch at the restaurant?
A. Put up the side curtains on the rented car.
Q. About what time was that?
A. I imagine we got there about twelve-fifteen.
Q. What time did you leave there?
A. It must have been one or a little after.

Q. When did you put up the side curtains?
A. Just before going in to eat.
Q. After you came out, what time did you get out of there?
A. We left after one.
Q. Then what did you do?
A. We drove to my home, and I put my car in the garage. Then we drove over to Ingleside Avenue, just south of the little alley south of 47th Street.
Q. What time did you put the car in the garage that day?
A. I should say at about one-twenty or one-thirty.
Q. In the afternoon?
A. Yes.
Q. And where was the other when you were putting your car in the garage?
A. The other car was right in the back of mine because we wanted to fill it with gas.
Q. In the area?
A. Yes.
Q. You brought that in and filled it up with gas, did you?
A. Yes, sir.
Q. And left your car there?

A. Yes, sir.
Q. Then what did you do?
A. Then we drove over to Ingleside Avenue, which is south of the alley, south of 47th Street.
Q. While you were filling the car up with gas, did you see anyone around the garage there?
A. I don't remember if Sven came down or not.
Q. Did you see Mr. Sven or Mrs. Sven there?
A. Mr. and Mrs. Englund. I am under the impression that Mr. Englund was there. I am not sure.
Chief Detective Michael Hughes: Q. You talked about the brakes being bad on that car?
A. Yes, on my car. It was on that occasion that they squeaked and should be oiled. He warned me about using them after they had been oiled.
Q. After you filled the car with gas, what did you do?
A. We drove to this spot on Ingleside Avenue.
Q. About what time?
A. It must have been a quarter of two.

Q. Then what did you do? You drove where you say?
A. To a point just south of the alley, south of 47th Street, Ingleside.
Q. You drove to a point which is south of the alley, south of 47th Street?
A. Yes, I waited in the car.
Q. On Ingleside?
A. On Ingleside.
Q. What is there, anything?
A. Apartment buildings. I waited in the car there while Dick went through the alley to a place where he could either command a view of Harvard School or if he saw any likely looking children, he could start playing with them.
After some time, I should say around three, several of the groups of boys played in the afternoon with the so-called tutors had left for a vacant lot on 49th and Drexel. We followed them up there, having made a stop at home for my field glasses in the meantime.
Q. What time was that?
A. Around three or three-fifteen. We parked on the opposite of Drexel Boulevard and watched these children at play. We also sneaked around on foot to a

point behind the lot, where we could observe without being seen. We also had another group of boys spotted in the lot just across the street from my home, 48th and Greenwood. We waited around until about a quarter of five, that is, four-thirty, I should say, when the gangs broke up, but one of the boys had run down the alley, as we thought, merely disappointed us. We missed our opportunity of following any of them home.

We then went down 41st and Lake Park Avenue, where an acquaintance of Richard's lived who had a son who might be expected home at that time.

Q. Do you remember the name?
A. Levinson.
Q. Do you know the address?
A. No, it is Sol Levinson, a lawyer, 41st and Lake Park. We repassed the lot on Greenwood, 48th and Greenwood, came over 48th Street to Ellis - no, we came over 49th Street to Ellis. It was 48th Street to Ellis, and here, Dick spied Robert Franks, who was at that time north of 48th Street on Ellis Avenue, on the west side of the street.

Q. You are sure it was on the west side of the street?
A. Positive. Walking south on the west side of the street.
Q. Then you were where, at that time?
A. We were on 48th and Ellis.
Q. On 48th or Ellis?
A. On 48th.
Q. Facing what direction?
A. West.
Q. On what side of the street would it be, on the east side?
A. We were driving down there. We immediately turned around, and about the time that we had turned around and given Robert a chance to get a sufficient distance from another pedestrian on the street, he was almost at 49th Street. It was here that we picked him up.
Q. You turned your car and started south on Ellis Avenue, is that it?
A. Yes, south on Ellis Avenue.
Q. On the west side of the street?
A. On the west side of the street.
Q. Robert Franks was at 49th?
A. He was almost at 49th.
Q. On Ellis?
A. Yes.

Q. Was he on the northwest corner, approximately?
A. Not quite, yes.
Q. You had not had a chance to cross?
A. No.
Q. And you drove up alongside of where he was?
A. Yes.
Q. And what happened?
A. Then Dick opened the front door and yelled, "Hey Bob!" He came over to the car, and Dick asked him if we couldn't give him a lift home. He declined, but Dick said, "Come in a minute. I want to talk to you about the tennis racket."
Q. That was the time he got into the car?
A. Yes.
Chief Detective Michael Hughes: Q. Where were you sitting at that time?
A. I was sitting at the driver's wheel. Dick was in the rear seat.
Q. What time was it approximately, Nathan?
A. Between five and five-fifteen.
Q. That was when you proceeded on your journey?
A. Yes.
Q. You went south, then to 50th Street?

A. South to 50th.
Q. And east on 59th?
A. East on 50th to, I believe, Dorchester or Blackstone.
Q. When was the first time that Richard struck Robert with the chisel, do you know?
A. Between Ellis and Greenwood, on 50th.
Q. Had he become suspicious of anything when you returned for him at that time?
A. No, because Richard asked him if he minded if we took him around the block, to which he replied no.
Q. That was the original plan, to take him so no one would see him?
A. Yes, sir.
Q. And after you made this trip out in the country and came back, what time did you get back?
A. Got back to where?
Q. To your home?
A. Ten-thirty.
Q. You still had the car that you had rented from the Rent-A-Car Company?
A. Yes, sir.

Q. Was that the car that you drove your folks home with?
A. No.
Q. What did you do with the rented car?
A. I parked it on Greenwood Avenue, just north of our driveway.
Q. On Greenwood Avenue?
A. On Greenwood Avenue.
Q. And you had your own car in the garage?
A. I got my own car in the garage and drove around to the side door.
Q. Then what did you do with your other car when you came back?
A. When I took Dick home - let me see, God, I think they were in my car because that chisel was thrown from my car, wasn't it? How could that have been accomplished? I am not quite clear on that point. But what he must have done was take the bundle - no, we didn't do that either because I remember washing the other car.
Q. That was the car that you rented?
A. Yes, we must have taken the rented car.
Q. That was after you got back?

A. Yes. I was around there until one o'clock.
Q. Where did Richard wait for you?
A. At my home.
Assistant State Attorney Joseph P. Savage: Q. What did you do with the rented car then?
A. Washed it fairly thoroughly there.
Q. When? That night?
A. One-thirty, yes.
Q. Whereabouts?
A. On 50th Street, at the gate to Loeb's.
Q. What did they wash it with?
A. We found a bucket with some water and a brush, and some soap.
Q. Where?
A. In Loeb's basement.
Q. Then you came out and washed it?
A. Yes, sir.
Q. You were unable to get the stains off?
A. Well, it was at night, and we didn't want to be monkeying around too much.
Q. Where did you take your car to get some of the bloodstains off?
A. No place.
Q. You drove the car in someplace to get some of the bloodstains off?
A. No. That was the next day in our

garage. It was still Wednesday night, you see.

Q. What did you do with the rented car that night?

A. I drove it back to the place previously occupied, which is just north of our driveway, stood in front of an apartment house.

Q. That was at one-thirty?

A. One-thirty.

Q. After you drove your aunt and uncle home in your car and came back, what did you do in the house then? Richard Loeb was in the house?

A. Went in and had a few drinks, sat, and talked with dad.

Q. What time was that about?

A. That must have been about eleven o'clock.

Q. Then what did you do?

A. Dad retired about eleven-thirty or twelve, and we had a few more drinks. Left about one o'clock.

Q. Did you play any cards while you were there?

A. Yes, I think we played two games of casino for fun.

Q. Then what did you do after that?

A. We went over to Dick's house with the clothes.
Q. The clothes in the rented car?
A. Yes, sir.
Q. And those were out in the rented car all the time?
A. Yes.
Q. In a robe?
A. In a robe.
Q. When you got to Dick's house, what did you do?
A. We went in the basement and burned the clothes. We intended burning the robe, but it was too large to fit in and would have caused an awful stench. Right after making that phone call to Franks, we were in the rented car. We drove over to Loeb's, then, in the rented car, burned the clothes, washed the bloodstains, then took the rented car to my house and left it there.
Then I got my car out, took the folks home in that. Then after I got back to my house, I still had that car. When I took Dick home, it was in that car. It was then we threw the chisel out.
Q. When you took Dick home, you took the rented car or your own car?

A. My own car.
Q. What actually happened there when you came in the first time?
A. We had disposed of the clothes.
Q. You had disposed of the clothes in the car?
A. Yes, sir.
Q. And left the robe hidden in the car?
A. No, I had left the robe hidden in some brush there.
Q. You mean outside?
A. Outdoors, yes.
Q. And Dick had the chisel in his possession?
A. Yes, sir.
Q. And when you changed cars, he just took it from one car to another with him?
A. Yes.
Q. Did he leave that in the car or not?
A. Yes.
Q. Did he leave that in the car or not?
A. I don't believe so, no.
Q. Where did he throw the chisel out at?
A. It was over there between 48th and, or between 49th and 50th, I think the latter, on Greenwood.
Q. After you left Richard there and came

back, you put your car in the garage, did you?
A. Yes, sir.
Q. Then what did you do?
A. I turned off the parking lights on the parked car and went to bed.
Q. Then what did you do?
A. Next morning I got up and went to school as usual at eight o'clock. I met Dick at eleven.
Q. Where?
A. At the University.
Q. You made arrangements the night before to meet the next day?
A. Yes, sir. We drove down to my house, and it was then that we drove the rented car to the garage to clean it up more thoroughly.
Q. In your garage?
A. Outside of my garage, but in my driveway.
Q. What did you clean it up with?
A. With soap and water and some gasoline, a brush.
Q. Did anyone help you clean it up?
A. Sven tried to, but we told him that was all right, that we were all through.
Chief Detective Michael Hughes: Q. Was

there any remarks made then with reference to the bloodstains in the car?
A. Yes, Dick was afraid that possibly Sven had seen these bloodstains, and he says it was some red wine.
Q. He told the chauffeur that?
A. Yes, sir.
Assistant State Attorney Joseph P. Savage: Q. Who drove the rented car downtown?
A. I drove the rented car downtown.
Q. And Dick drove your car, did he?
A. Dick drove my car.
Q. Then you went down and how much did you pay, do you remember, for the use of the car?
A. This was Thursday, was it?
Q. Yes.
A. Wait just a minute. We cleaned the car out. Where did we eat that day? I have forgotten where we ate. We stopped someplace for lunch, and we didn't have my car at all. We both drove the rented car.
Q. You didn't have your car at all?
A. No, my car was in the garage, and we drove down to the 12th Street Illinois Central Station, and the rest of the account is contained in the previous part.

Q. With the rented car?
A. Yes, sir.
Q. When did you return the rented car?
A. We returned the rented car at about five or five-thirty.
Q. How much money?
A. Twenty-five dollars and some cents on it.
Q. And he gave you the balance of your deposit back?
A. Yes, sir.
Chief Detective Michael Hughes: Q. You drove the rented car, both of you, to the I.C. station?
A. Yes, and then drove back south. After we had found that Mr. Franks was not at the drugstore, we drove to my house, got my car, and Dick drove my car down while I drove the rented car down. Dick parked on Wabash Avenue just south of 14th Street while I returned the car.
Assistant State Attorney Joseph P. Savage: Q. About what time was that?
A. Between five-fifteen and five-thirty. When we returned, we stopped to get a soda at the drugstore.
Q. Whereabouts?

A. 47th and Ellis. I met Mr. Mitchell at that time.
Q. You had a conversation with him?
A. I had a conversation with him. I took Dick home, on the way back, stopped, and bought a paper at 48th and Ellis, which told about the fact that this boy was Franks, and went home.
Q. Then what happened?
A. I got supper. I stayed at home studying law.
Q. Did you see Dick the next day?
A. The next day was Friday, yes.
Q. Was that the time you had the conversation of what you would say in the event you were called in?
A. I am not sure if it was then or not. We discussed that a number of times.
Q. Prior to the happening or after the happening?
A. Possibly after that time. I could not be sure.
Q. You discovered there was a pair of glasses found out there, Nathan?
A. Yes.
Q. You learned that through a newspaper?
A. Yes.

Q. Then you and Richard Loeb had some conversation about the glasses, and so forth?
A. Yes, sir.
Q. You contemplated at that time that you would be called in and asked about it?
A. Yes, sir.
Q. In the event they were found. You never thought they would find the owner of the glasses, did you?
A. No, I did not.
Q. You were called in by...?
A. Captain Wolfe.
Q. What did Captain Wolfe ask you?
A. Captain Wolfe wanted to know whether I had visited the particular area frequently, whether there were many ornithologists whom I knew or firemen, particularly among the members of the Harvard School or its faculty. Also, whether the Franks boy had been interested.
Q. You gave him the information?
A. Yes.
Q. Did you mention the fact to him at that time that you had worn glasses?
A. Yes.

Q. He never asked you to produce your glasses?
A. No.
Q. This wine that Richard told us about, were you able to remove all those bloodstains?
A. Almost entirely.
Q. Enough so that it was not noticeable?
A. Yes.
Q. What time was it, Nathan, now, when you saw the newspapers announcing that?
A. About six o'clock.
Q. This chisel that was thrown out of the car by Richard that you told about, Nathan, that had what kind of tape on it?
A. Zinc oxide.
Q. Where did you get the tape at, from home?
A. In the bathroom.
Q. This was the tape you were telling me about that your brother had in the bathroom when you walked in?
A. Yes.
Q. Did you take a whole roll of it?
A. Yes.
Q. Where did you leave the rest of it?

A. We have discussed that, Dick and I, and we think it must have been in the car.
Q. Did you put the tape on near the sharp end or the blunt end?
A. The sharp end.
Q. Using the head of the chisel or the blunt end, I guess you call it, for the purpose of?
A. Striking.
Q. Which end did Richard strike with, do you know? Did he strike with the sharp end or the other end?
A. He struck with the other end. That's why I can't explain the bloodstains. Well, probably the bleeding was rather effusive.
Q. You don't know whether it was the other end or not, did you?
A. Yes, I do.
Chief Detective Michael Hughes: Q. Where did the chisel come from?
A. From a hardware store between 45th and 46th, on Cottage Grove Avenue.
Assistant State Attorney Joseph P. Savage: Q. Who bought the chisel?
A. Dick.
Q. That same day?

A. No, I think we bought that a few days previously.
Q. For that purpose?
A. Yes, sir.
Q. As the hardware store, where?
A. 45th and 46th, on Cottage.
Q. Do you remember what you paid for it?
A. I think it was seventy-five cents.
Q. Which one of you bought it?
A. Dick.
Q. You bought that two or three days before?
A. I think so, yes.
Q. How did you carry it around with you?
A. As I recollect, we put it in the pocket of the rented car. I think we bought that on the very day, on Wednesday the 21st. I am almost sure of that now.
Q. The same day?
A. Yes, sir.
Q. That was the day you went in and got the tape in the house?
A. Yes.
Q. Now, the time you started wearing the glasses was when Nathan?
A. In October or November 1923.

Q. And who was your doctor that prescribed the glasses?
A. Emil Deutsch.
Q. And he is located where?
A. 30 North Michigan.
Q. And the one who filled the prescription?
A. Almer Coe.
Q. How long did you wear the glasses, Nathan, afterward?
A. Until February or March.
Q. 1924?
A. 1924.
Q. Then you sort of discontinued wearing them, is that it?
A. Yes, sir. They did actually remain in the pocket of the suit that they had been, which happened to be this suit.
Q. The suit you have got on now is the suit you wore the night you placed the body there, is that it?
A. Yes, sir.
Q. After you started out there, Nathan, did you remove your clothes at all while you were placing the body?
A. My coat, yes.
Q. Just how did you place the body in the

drainpipe? Just explain how you placed the body in there.
A. I think it was headfirst. I had a pair of rubber boots.
Q. Where did you get the rubber boots?
A. My own.
Q. Did you take them from your house?
A. Yes.
Q. That day in this rented car, did you?
A. Yes, put them on right at the culvert. There, I stepped into the water, took the feet of the body while Dick took the head end and the hands, and when it struck the water, pushed it in, gave it a shove as far as I could.
Q. Was it much of a job, Nathan, to push the body in?
A. At first, I thought it was rather doubtful whether it would fit at all, but after it once started, it wasn't hard at all.
Q. Then, after you pushed it in as far as you could push it in with your hands, Nathan, you used your feet to push it up further?
A. Yes, sir.
Q. Had rigor mortis set in at that time?
A. Yes.
Q. At the time you had taken your coat

off, did you lay it on the ground someplace?
A. Yes, right by my shoes.
Q. That isn't the time you lost your glasses?
A. No, that isn't the time. Dick had run across the railroad track to see if anybody could be seen from the other end, and I went up to the top of the railroad track for some reason or other to put on my shoes, and he brought my coat to me. I think we struck a match. No, we had a flashlight with us, and it must have been at that time that the glasses fell out.
Q. What time was it, again, that you put the body in the drain?
A. About nine-thirty. Nine-thirty or nine-twenty.
Q. Dick brought your coat up to you where you were putting on your shoes?
A. Yes.
Q. Now, this letter, Nathan, that you had already prepared, in an envelope without any address on it, you had prepared that letter sometime prior to that time?
A. Yes.
Q. Just when did you prepare that letter?
A. Four or five days ahead of time.

THE CONFESSION OF NATHAN LEOPOLD | 139

Q. No one definitely as to who you were going to send it to?
A. No, just "Dear Sir."
Q. But the address you placed on later on?
A. Yes. It wasn't addressed inside. It was just "Dear Sir."
Q. You didn't send that additional letter that was supposed to be sent about committing suicide?
A. No.
Q. Did you ever send a special letter?
A. No, sir.
Q. Or make any calls after what you have told us about?
A. No, sir.
Q. Those shoes and belt, you say, Nathan, were placed on what road?
A. On a little spur road up the road leading to Gary from Calumet Boulevard.
Q. In the woods there, is that it?
A. It is near the Russian Orthodox Cemetery.
Q. What kind of acid was that you say you used?
A. Hydrochloric.
Q. On the face and body?

A. Yes, sir.
Q. Does it take some time for that to take action?
A. Apparently, it must.
Q. Evidently, it didn't take any action at all?
A. There was a faint discoloration noticed.
Chief Detective Michael Hughes: Q. Did the poison get into the mouth, do you know?
A. It probably did.
Q. Where did you administer the poison on him?
A. At the culvert there.
Q. What did you do with the bottle that contained the poison?
A. I think we took the bottle with us, whether we left it in the rented car or threw it out on the way home, I don't know.
Q. Your purpose for doing that was to disfigure the face and body so it would not be recognized?
A. So, it would not be recognized immediately.
Q. You told us what drugstore you called up when you called Franks?
A. The first time, you mean?

Q. Yes, that night, at 12:30. That was the drugstore at 4th and Woodlawn.
A. Yes, sir.
Q. Was Dick with you?
A. Yes.
Assistant State Attorney Joseph P. Savage: Q. Was he inside or outside?
A. We were both in the telephone booth.
Q. Did you always do the talking on the phone?
A. Yes. My voice is considerably lower-pitched than Dick's, and Dick's is more distinct over the phone.
Chief Detective Michael Hughes: Q. What drugstore did you call from when you called the drugstore on 63rd Street to see whether Mr. Franks was there?
A. It was from Walgreen's drugstore on the corner of 67th and Stony Island Avenue, and then from a drugstore on the southwest corner of 68th and Stony Island Avenue.
Q. Where was the place that you selected where he was to throw the box out?
A. At 74th Street and the I.C. tracks.
Q. There is a factory there that is just the same as you described?
A. Yes, you couldn't miss it.

Q. And you were to be there, you and Richard were to be there at the time the box was to be thrown out?
A. Yes.
Q. What became of the ticket that Richard bought for Gary?
A. He bought a ticket, and we talked about trying to cash the ticket in again. But it had been punched, and we decided to tear them both up.
Q. Did you buy two tickets?
A. No, just one.
Q. Who wrote the letter that Richard dropped in the mailbox in the car?
A. Who wrote the letter?
Q. Yes.
A. You mean who typed it or who composed it?
Q. Who typed it?
A. I wrote it.
Q. On the same machine?
A. On the same machine.
Q. Do you remember how it read?
A. "Dear Sir"
Q. It was addressed to Mr. Franks on the outside?
A. Yes, Mr. Franks. On the inside, it read, "Dear Sir: Proceed immediately to the

THE CONFESSION OF NATHAN LEOPOLD

rear platform of the train. Have your package ready, face the east immediately after you have passed the first large red brick factory with a black water tower, with the wording "Champion" in white on it. Count three or four...." I don't know just what it was, "....then throw the package as far as you can. Your son will be delivered to you within six hours after our receipt of the money." Signed "George Johnson."

Q. That was also mentioned in the letter that you wrote to Franks?

A. The one of six hours?

Q. Yes.

A. Then it wasn't in this letter. I thought it was this letter.

Assistant State Attorney Joseph P. Savage: Q. You have not been abused in any way by anyone?

A. No, sir.

Chief Detective Michael Hughes: Q. Let me ask you this, was there any blood on Richard's clothes?

A. Yes, sir.

Q. What became of the clothing?

A. He scrubbed it, so it didn't show.

Q. Is that the suit he is wearing?

A. No.
Q. He has got a very light gray?
A. No, that isn't the one. It was more of a greenish-gray suit.
Q. Where did he wash the stains off?
A. At home.
Q. In the basement?
A. No.
Q. Where?
A. Upstairs, after I left, finally. After I finally took him home.
Q. That night?
A. That night.
Q. Were his folks in bed?
A. Yes.
Q. Has he worn those clothes since?
A. Yes.
Assistant State Attorney Joseph P. Savage: Q. Did you have any blood on your clothes?
A. I had only very, very small stains.
Q. Where was that?
A. On the back of my coat.
Q. How did you take it off?
A. Soaked it off.
Q. You at no time struck Robert Franks at all?
A. No, sir.
Q. You at no time choked him?

THE CONFESSION OF NATHAN LEOPOLD | 145

A. No, sir.
Q. At the time you conceived kidnapping some young fellow around there, did you intend to murder him? What was your intention to murder him first and hide the body?
A. No, we intended to murder him.
Q. Your intentions were to murder him and hide the body and collect the money afterward?
A. Yes.
Q. That was the general plan?
A. Yes.
Q. Why did you conceive that idea? Why did you intend to murder him?
A. Because he couldn't expose us.
Q. What did you intend to do with the money, the ten thousand dollars, when you collected it?
A. Hide it away, either in a safety deposit box or some other safe place, for a year, and then spend it very carefully.
Q. That was the agreement reached between you and Richard?
A. Yes.
Q. When Richard hit Robert first, was it down in the tonneau of the car, the

bottom of the car, or was it on the east he choked him?

A. It was on the east. Robert was sitting in the front seat. Dick was in the back seat.

Q. Robert was sitting in the front with you?

A. Yes, and Dick sort of leaned over and put his hand over his mouth, like this.

Q. Did he pull him back in the rear?

A. Not until later.

Q. After he cracked him on the head, did he fall down then, Robert?

A. No, he struggled.

Q. Now then, since you have been here with the Chief and the Assistant State's Attorney and the other police officers, no one has abused you in any way, have they?

A. No, sir.

PART III

JUDGMENT DAY

5

TRIAL, PSYCH & SENTENCE

Outside the court during the trial

TRIAL

One thing that hasn't changed in the American legal system is that you will get the trial afforded to you. In the case of both Leopold and Loeb, this would be a lot. Since both came from prominent, well-to-do families, they would have only the best in their legal defense. The "best" would be Clarence Darrow and Benjamin Bachrach.

Even though Darrow was born in the small town of Farmdale, Ohio, he had become known as the "Sophisticated Country Lawyer." When he first moved to Chicago, he joined the Democratic Party, which gave him some affluent contacts. Likely, this is where he learned to be such a great speaker. His deliveries were made with such a passion he would often leave many in the crowd in tears.

Darrow's first murder case was in 1894 when he defended Patrick Eugene Prendergast, who had confessed to murdering the then-mayor of Chicago Carter Harrison. Darrow wasn't successful in proving that Prendergast was insane, as he was convicted and later executed for the murder. However, Darrow's record for defending murderers changed after he saved both Leopold and Loeb from the death penalty in this murder case.

Along with his political affiliation in the early nineteen hundreds, Darrow was primarily a corporate and labor lawyer when he tried running as a congressional candidate for the Democratic Party. His most well-known clients included the American Federation of Labor, Western Federation of Miners, the Woodworkers of Wisconsin, and the United Mine Workers of Pennsylvania.

Darrow wasn't without public scandal before the Leopold and Loeb trial. In early 1912, Darrow was charged with two counts of attempting to bribe jurors in two cases while working as the defense lawyer in California. Both trials were lengthy and got a lot of attention from the media. In one case, he was acquitted, and the other ended in a hung jury. The prosecutor made an agreement with Darrow not to retry him as long as Darrow promised not to practice law again in the state of California.

Because these bribery charges were so public, most unions and corporations wanted to distance themselves from Darrow and would no longer hire him for any of their litigations. This situation made Darrow switch to civil law, where he started to defend criminal cases for regular citizens. Darrow held a strong belief that the death penalty was wrong and actively looked to death penalty cases so that he could stop the 'murders of citizens by the government,' as he called it. His belief was not a popular stance back in the early twentieth century.

In the summer of 1924, Darrow jumped at the opportunity to defend what Chicago newspapers called the "Trial of the Century." Not only was he excited to try and save these two teenage boys from certain death, but he was also estimated to have been paid several million dollars from the parents of the two charged with the murder.

As both Leopold and Loeb confessed to the kidnapping and murder of Bobby Franks and they pled guilty, it wasn't going to be a trial, but more like a hearing. Before Darrow came on to the case, the boys had pled not guilty. They had hoped to be declared insane, therefore, not to be executed. After Darrow started on the case, he had them change their pleas to guilty. Darrow did this primarily so that a judge and not a jury would do the sentencing. It was reported that he did this when he found out the judge was John R. Caverly, who was known as someone who also didn't like the death penalty. Darrow also told the press that "When responsibility is divided by twelve, it is easy to say away with him." But with a judge, Darrow said, "Your Honor, if these boys are to hang, you must do it. It must be by your cool, premeditated act."

Darrow's main goal was to save the boys from being executed. Therefore, he had to get the best alienists, the psychiatrists of that time, to convince the judge that the mental disease that both Leopold and Loeb had should be a mitigating factor in their sentencing.

The prosecution disagreed with that premise and asked the judge not to use such evidence since whether they were insane or not was only imperative in sentencing a murder case but only used for determining sanity. The judge agreed with Darrow and decided to allow the testimony of the alienists.

After that decision, the race was on to get the most famous and smartest alienists to testify for the prosecution and defense. Darrow preplanned this strategy right down to the judge and his decision. Consequently, he had already contacted all of the best alienists worldwide, including Sigmund Freud. Freud initially agreed to come and examine Leopold and Loeb but became very ill and unable to travel, so he didn't appear.

The upcoming trial became a conversation piece for everyone in Chicago and the rest of the United States. As such, the fact that both Leopold and Loeb were from prominent families who were spending millions of dollars on the defense soon turned into a problem for Darrow. Many regular Americans became angry that these two spoiled murdering kids might get away with their crime because they had money.

Darrow's reported fee for the defense was around $200,000. Yet, according to the 1957 book *Attorney for the Damned* by A. Weinberg, Darrow received $70,000 for his fee. This amount included his expenses, which were close to $40,000, leaving Darrow with only about $30,000.

Darrow did get fame from the Leopold and Loeb defense trial, though. In 1925, he was hired to defend John T. Scopes, one of the major trials in American justice history. The Scopes trial was a challenge against the law that made it illegal to teach the 'Evolution Theory' in any state school or university. That law also made it illegal for them to present any theory that denied the 'Divine Creation' story from the Christian Bible. This law hints at the conservative nature of the country and its adults. They not only had stopped the production and sale of alcohol, prevented schools from teaching anything outside of the creation theory in the Bible, but were also supportive of the death penalty. All of which stacked public opinion against Clarence Darrow and his clients.

On top of that, the *Chicago Daily Tribune*, the largest circulated paper in Chicago and one of the largest Hearst newspapers in the country, was running a daily poll to see if they should broadcast the Leopold and Loeb trial on their radio station WGN in Chicago. Ultimately, the survey voted not to broadcast the trial. But only by a few percentage points. It was nearly a 50/50 split.

It's been reported that the State's Attorney Robert Crowe started this poll in the conservative paper, intending to keep people discussing the case daily. But more importantly, he believed that broadcasting the details to the public would be helpful to him in getting the death penalty.

Robert Crowe was the complete opposite of Darrow. He was a firm believer in the Bible and constantly quoted scriptures. When asked about this case, one of his most famous sayings was, "The hand of God is at work in this case." He later became a judge and became known for sentencing almost every person that he convicted to death.

PSYCH

Darrow tried to convince the Judge that both Leopold and Loeb had no control over their actions. His alienists' testimony proved that both boys suffered severe mental trauma during their childhood – trauma that damaged their ability to function competently and emotionally.

His most crucial witness about this subject was Dr. William White, considered the best psychologist of that time. Even President Theodore Roosevelt appointed White to be the Superintendent of the Government Hospital for the Insane.

White suggested that Leopold and Loeb had such horrible experiences as young children that they would have superstitious compulsions and paranoid thoughts, leading to hallucinations and fantasies. Both were emotionally immature, and by their early adulthood, they were antisocial.

Leopold was so lonely from his miserable childhood at home, and by having no friends, he relied entirely on his intellect for survival and ignored all emotions, figuring they were useless. White considered Loeb as having infantilism, or still a little child emotionally, who still thought his childhood teddy bear to be his confidant and continued to talk to it right up until the murder of Franks.

Another vital witness to testify and help support White's claims was Dr. Bernard Glueck, who had previously treated the criminally insane prisoners at Sing Sing Prison. Glueck actually went even further with his diagnosis of Leopold by calling him Schizophrenic. This condition left Leopold unable to make decisions. Glueck believed that Leopold was so wrapped up living in his fantasies that he practically had no free will of his own.

One of Leopold's regular fantasies was being a slave to somebody very important and powerful, such as a king or ruler of some country. His need to be indispensable to that king or ruler was the most important thing for him to achieve. He believed it would make him feel worthy or valuable. Usually, he had inferior feelings about himself both as a person and sexually.

Below are some highlights from Glueck's testimony. Benjamin Bachrach was Clarence Darrow's co-counsel.

Bernard Glueck (psychiatrist): I then took up with Loeb the Franks' crime and asked him to tell me about it. He recited to me in a most matter-of-fact way all the gruesome details of the planning and execution of this crime, of the disfiguring and the disposal of the body, how he and Leopold stopped with the body in the car to get something to eat on the way.

He spoke to me in the most matter-of-factly way about his doings and movements immediately following this act. As his recital proceeded, I was amazed at the absolute absence of any signs of normal feeling, such as one would expect under the circumstances.

He showed no remorse, no regret, no compassion for the people involved in this situation, and as he kept on talking, there became evident the absolute lack of normal human emotional response that would fit these situations, and the whole thing became incomprehensible to me except on the basis of a disordered personality.

In the course of my conversation with him, he told me how his little brother passed in review before him as a possible victim of the kidnapping and killing. Even in connection with this statement, he showed the same lack of adequate emotional response to the situation.

Benjamin Bachrach: In the conversation with Richard Loeb, did he say anything about who it was that struck the blow on the head of Robert Franks with the chisel?

Bernard Gluek: He told me all the details of the crime, including the fact that he struck the blow.

Benjamin Bachrach: If you have reached

any conclusion with reference to his mental condition, you may now state it.

Bernard Gluek: My impression is very definite that this boy is suffering from a disordered personality, that the nature of this disorder is primarily in a profound pathological discord between his intellectual and emotional life.

Benjamin Bachrach: Now then, doctor, are you ready to begin with your examination of the defendant Nathan F. Leopold Jr.?

Bernard Gluek: Yes.

Benjamin Bachrach: You may proceed.

Bernard Gluek: I started out with him by asking him to tell me about the Franks' murder. He argued with me that for many years he has cultivated and adhered to a purely hedonistic philosophy – that all action is justified if it gives pleasure. That was his ambition and has been for many years to become a perfect Nietzschean and to follow Nietzsche's philosophy all the way through.

He told me of his attitude toward Loeb and of how completely he had put himself in the role of a slave in connection with him. He said, "I can illustrate it to you by saying that I felt myself less than the dust beneath his feet." He told me of his abject devotion to Loeb, saying that he was jealous of the food and drink that Loeb took because he could not come as close to him as did the food and drink.

Nathan F. Leopold, in my estimation, is a definitely paranoid personality, perhaps developing a definite paranoid psychosis. I have not seen a definite psychosis of this sort in as young a person as he is. His aberration is characterized primarily by this abnormal pathological transformation of his personality and by the delusional way of thinking.

Benjamin Bachrach: Doctor, from your experience in dealing with persons of a disordered mind state, is it common and ordinary to find in such persons a high degree of intelligence existing at the same time as the abnormality or diseased condition?

Bernard Gluek: If I should give an answer to this question in a general way, I should say that it is quite characteristic of paranoid individuals to have, along with their disordered mental state, a highly developed intelligence.

Benjamin Bachrach: Have you observed among other such persons under your care the ability to plan like ordinary intelligent people without abnormality?

Bernard Gluek: I have observed the most ingenious and great capacity to plan among paranoid patients. Patients suffering from mental disorder and 90 percent of my patients in private practice do suffer from mental disorders carry on their activities while they are under treatment for their mental disorder.

Even though Crowe was able to find four fairly reputable alienists to testify that neither Leopold nor Loeb had any mental diseases or derangement, the judge believed that both boys had shown some mental and emotional conditions.

Crowe's best testimony came from his witness Dr. William Healy, known as the leader of the "Child Guidance Movement." Some of the highlights of William Healy's testimony from the trial are below.

Clarence Darrow: What did you learn about the relationship between Leopold and Loeb?

William Healy: As far as I can find out from the account given by the boys themselves and from their relatives, their association began at fifteen years of age. They just barely knew each other earlier, but that is the time they first came together. It is very clear from the study of the boys separately that each came with peculiarities in their mental life.

Each arrived at these peculiarities by different routes; each supplemented the others already constituted abnormal needs in a most unique way. And in regard to the association, I think that the crime in its commission and in its background has features that are quite beyond anything in my experience or knowledge of the literature.

There seems to have been so little normal motivation. The matter was so long-planned, so unfeelingly carried out, that it represents nothing that I have ever seen or heard of before.

In the matter of the association, I have the boys' story, told separately, about an incredibly absurd childish compact that bound them.

For Loeb, he says, the association gave him the opportunity of getting someone to carry out his criminalistic imaginings and conscious ideas. In the case of Leopold, the direct cause of his entering into criminalistic acts was this particularly childish compact.

Robert Crowe: You are talking about a compact that you characterize as childish. Kindly tell us what that compact was.

William Healy: I am perfectly willing to

tell it in chambers, but it is not a matter that I think should be told here.

Robert Crowe: I insist that we know what that compact is so that we can form some opinion about it. Tell it in court. The trial must be public, your Honor. I am not insisting that he talk loud enough for everybody to hear, but it ought to be told in the same way that we put the other evidence in.

After a discussion with the attorneys at the bench, Judge Caverly told William Healy to whisper his answers so that only the judge, the attorneys, and the stenographers could hear his words.

William Healy: This compact, as was told to me separately by each of the boys, consisted in an agreement between them that Leopold, who has very definite homosexual tendencies, was to have the privilege of... Do you want me to be very specific?

Robert Crowe: Absolutely, because this is important.

William Healy: Was to have the privilege of inserting his penis between Loeb's legs at special rates. At one time, it was to be three times in two months if they continued their criminalistic activities together. Then, they had some of their quarrels, and then it was once for each criminalistic deed.

Clarence Darrow: I do not suppose this should be taken in the presence of newspapermen, your Honor.

Judge Caverly: Gentlemen, will you go and sit down, you newspapermen! Take your seats. This should not be published.

Robert Crowe: What other acts, if any, did they tell you about? You say that there are other acts that they did rarely or seldom?

William Healy: Oh, they were just experimenting once or twice with each other.

Clarence Darrow: Tell what it was.

William Healy: They experimented with mouth perversions. Leopold has had for many years a great deal of fantasy life surrounding sex activity. He has fantasies of being with a man, and usually with Loeb himself. He says he gets a thrill out of anticipating it. Loeb would pretend to be drunk, then this fellow would undress him, and he would almost rape him and would be furiously passionate. With women, he does not get that same thrill and passion.

Robert Crowe: That is what he tells you?

William Healy: Surely. That is what he tells me. Loeb tells me himself how he sometimes feigns to be drunk in order that he should have his aid in carrying out his criminalistic ideas. That is what Leopold gets out of it, and that is what Loeb gets out of it.

When Leopold had this first experience with his penis between Loeb's legs, he found it gave him more pleasure than anything else he had ever done. Even in jail here, a look at Loeb's body or his touch upon his shoulder thrills him so, he says, immeasurably.

Robert Crowe: When Leopold began to plan with Loeb this murder, what was acting then, his intellect or his emotions?

William Healy: His intellect. But always accompanied by some emotional life, as it always is.

Robert Crowe: Which was in control, the intellect or the emotions at the time they planned to steal the typewriter so that they could write letters that could not be traced back to them?

William Healy: I think the intellect was the predominating thing there probably.

Robert Crowe: And when they rented the room in the Morrison Hotel, intellect was still walking in front?

William Healy: Yes.

Robert Crowe: And so on through all the details of this murder?

William Healy: Yes, sir.

After the psychological testimonies ended, the prosecution had two letters read into evidence.

LETTER #1: From Nathan Leopold to Richard Loeb, dated October 9th, 1923

"Dear Dick:

In view of our former relations, I take it for granted that it is unnecessary to make any excuse for writing to you at this time, and still am going to state my reasons for doing so, as this may turn out to be a long letter, and I don't want to cause you the inconvenience of reading it all to find out what it contains if you are not interested in the subjects dealt with.

First, I am enclosing the document which I mentioned to you today and which I will explain later. Second, I am going to tell you of a new fact which has come up since our discussion.

And third, I am going to put in writing what my attitude is toward our present relations, with a view of avoiding future misunderstandings, and in the hope (which I think is rather vain) that possibly we may have misunderstood each other and can yet clear this matter up.

Now, as to the first, I wanted you this afternoon, and still want you, to feel that we are on equal footing legally, and, therefore, I purposely committed the same tort of which you were guilty, the only difference being that in your case the facts would be harder to prove than in mine, should I deny them. The enclosed document should secure you against changing my mind in admitting the facts if the matter should come up, as it would prove to any court that they were true.

As to the second - on your suggestion, I immediately phoned Dick Rubel, and speaking from a paper prepared beforehand (to be sure of exact wording), said: "Dick when we were together yesterday, did I tell you that Dick (Loeb) had told me the things which I then told you, or that it was merely my opinion that I believed them to be so?" I asked this twice to be sure he understood, and on the same answer, both times (which I took down as he spoke) felt that he did understand. He replied: "No, you did not tell me that Dick told you these things but said that they were, in your opinion, true."

He further denied telling you subsequently that I had said that they were gleaned from a conversation with you, and I then told him that he was quite right, that you had never told me. I further told him that this was merely your suggestion of how to settle a question of fact, that he was in no way implicated, and that neither of us would be angry with him at his reply. (I imply your assent to this.) This, of course, proves that you were mistaken this afternoon in the question of my having actually and technically broken confidence and voids my apology, which I made contingent on proof of this matter.

Now, as to the third, last, and most important question. When you came to my home this afternoon, I expected either to break friendship with you or attempt to kill you, unless you told me why you acted as you did yesterday. You did, however, tell me, and hence the question shifted to the fact that I would act as before if you persisted in thinking me treacherous, either in act (which you waived if Dick's opinion went with mine) or in intention.

Now, I apprehend, though here I am not quite sure, that you said that you did not think *me treacherous in intent, nor ever have, but that you considered me in the wrong and expected such a statement from me. This statement I unconditionally refused to make until such time as I may have become convinced of its truth.*

However, the question of our relation, I think, must be in your hands (unless the above conceptions are mistaken) inasmuch as you have satisfied first one and then the other requirement, upon which I agreed to refrain from attempting to kill you or refusing to continue our friendship. Hence, I have no reason not to continue to be on friendly terms with you and would, under ordinary conditions, continue as before.

The only question, then, is with you. You demand me to perform an act, namely, state that I acted wrongly. This I refuse. Now it is up to you to inflict the penalty for this refusal-at your discretion, to break friendship, inflict physical punishment, or anything else you like, or on the other hand, continue as before. The decision, therefore, must rest with you. This is all of my opinion on the right and wrong of the matter.

Now comes a practical question. I think that I would ordinarily be expected to, and in fact do expect to continue my attitude toward you, as before, until I learn either by direct words or by conduct on your part which way your decision has been formed. This I shall do.

Now a word of advice. I do not wish to influence your decision either way, but I do want to warn you that in case you deem it advisable to discontinue our friendship, that in both our interests, extreme care must be had. The motif of "A falling out of a pair of cocksuckers" would be sure to be popular, which is patently undesirable and forms an irksome but unavoidable bond between us. Therefore, it is, in my humble opinion, expedient, though our breach need be no less real in fact, yet to observe the conventionalities, such as salutation on the street and a general appearance of at least not unfriendly relations on all occasions when we may be thrown together in public.

Now, Dick, I am going to make a request to which I have perhaps no right, and yet which I dare to make also for "Auld Lang Syne." Will you, if not too inconvenient, let me know your answer (before I leave tomorrow) on the last count? This, to which I have no right, would greatly help my peace of mind in the next few days when it is most necessary to me. You can, if you will, merely call up my home before 12 noon and leave a message saying, "Dick says yes," if you wish our relations to continue as before, and "Dick says no," if not.

It is unnecessary to add that your decision will, of course, have no effect on my keeping to myself our confidences of the past and that I regret the whole affair more than I can say.

Hoping not to have caused you too much trouble in reading this, I am (for the present) as ever.

Babe"

The enclosure that was included with this letter read:

"I, Nathan F. Leopold Jr., being under no duress or compulsion, do hereby affirm and declare that on this, the 9th day of October 1923, I for reasons of my own locked the door of the room in which I was with one Richard A. Loeb, with the intent of blocking his only feasible mode of egress, and that I further indicated my intention of applying physical force upon the person of the said Richard A. Loeb if necessary to carry out my design, to-wit, to block his only feasible mode of egress."

LETTER #2: From Nathan Leopold to Richard Loeb
Toledo, Ohio
Addressed to Mr. Richard A. Loeb
5107 Ellis Avenue, Chicago
a special delivery letter
October 10, 20th Century Limited, 1:45 p.m.

"Dear Dick:

I want to thank you first of all for your kindness in granting my request yesterday. I was highly gratified to hear from you for two reasons, the first sentimental and the second practical. The first of these is that your prompt reply conclusively proved my previous idea that the whole matter really did mean something to you and that you respected my wishes, even though we were not very friendly. This is a great satisfaction, but the second is even greater, in that I imply from the general tenor of your letter that there is a good chance of a reconciliation between us, which I ardently desire, and this belief will give me a peace of mind on which I based my request.

But I fear, Dick, that your letter has failed to settle the controversy itself, as two points are still left open. These I will now attack. As I wrote you yesterday, the decision of our relations was in your hands because it depended entirely on how you wished to treat my refusal to admit that I acted wrongly. This request you did not answer. You imply merely that because of my statement that "I regret the whole matter," I am in part at least admitting what you desire. I thought twice before putting that phrase in my letter for fear you might misconstrue it, as in fact, you have done.

First, you will note that I said that "I regret the whole matter" (not any single part of it). By this, I meant that I regretted the crime you originally committed (your mistake in judgment) from which the whole consequences flow. But I did not mean and do not wish to understand as meaning that once this act had been done, I regret anything subsequent. I do not, in fact, regret it because I feel sure, as I felt from the beginning, that should we again become friends, it will be on the basis of better mutual understanding as a result of these unpleasant consequences which I deliberately planned and precipitated.

Furthermore, even if I did not regret those consequences, it would not follow at all that I consider myself to have acted wrongly. I may regret that it is necessary to go downtown to the dentist and still not feel that I am acting wrongly in so doing – quite the contrary. So, if you insist on my stating that I acted wrongly as a prerequisite to our renewal of friendship, I feel it duty-bound to point out to you that this is not the meaning of what I wrote. In this, do not think that I am trying to avoid a renewal of these relations. You know how much I desire a renewal, but I still feel that I must point this out to you, as I could not consider re-entering these relations when you were under the misapprehensions that I had conceded to what you demanded. On the basis of this construction of my words, then, Dick, should you base your decision.

Next comes the other point of issue, namely, whether I wish to be a party to a reconciliation, supposing that you wish on the basis of the previous statements to do so. Here, the decisions rest, not with you, but with me. Now, as I wrote you yesterday, you obviated my first reason for a refusal by telling me what I wanted to know, but another arose, the question of treachery, and that is not quite settled in my mind. For the purpose of this discussion, I shall not use the short-term "treachery" as you suggested in your letter to cover whatever you want to call it. I have no desire to quibble over terms and am sure we both mean the same thing as treachery. Very well.

The whole question must be divided into two, namely, treachery in act and treachery in intention. On your suggestion, the first was to be settled by phoning Dick, as I did. I apologized verbally on the condition that you were right and implying the same apology from you in case you were wrong.

You were proved wrong, and I am sure you are a good enough sport to stick by your statement unless you question whether I did all you suggested in good faith. Hence, you remove any previous charge of treachery in the act — if there was such. But the second is not so simple. I stated, and still hold, that if you still held me to have acted treacherously in intent, our friendship must cease. You circumvent that by saying you could never have held this opinion because you believe me to have acted hastily, etc. I did my best in stating I was wholly responsible for all I said and did since I had planned it all, and if there were malice at all, it would be a malice afterthought. You refuse to believe me. Now, that is not my fault.

I have done my best to tell you the true facts (since they were to my disadvantage) and hence have discharged my obligation. I still insist that I have planned all I did. You can believe this or not as you like or come to your own decision, or whether you still think I acted treacherously. If you say you do not, then I shall infer either that you never thought so (although you accuse me of it) or that you have changed your mind (and imply these as an apology for ever thinking so) and continue to be your friend. All I want from you then is a statement; that you do not now think me to have acted treacherously in intent, which I will construe as above. Then it is up to you whether you will forego my statement of the wrong action or will, on your part, break up our friendship.

Please wire me at my expense to the Biltmore Hotel, New York, immediately on receipt, stating, one, whether you wish to "break our friendship" or to forego my statement, or, two, whether or not you still think me to have acted treacherously. If you want further discussion on either point, merely wire me that you must see me, to discuss it before you decide.

Now, that is all that is in point to our controversy, but I am going to ask a little more in an effort to explain my system of Nietzschean philosophy with regard to you.

It may have occurred to you why a mere

mistake in judgment on your part should be treated as a crime when on the part of another, it should not be so considered. Here are the reasons. In formulating a superman, he is, on account of certain superior qualities inherent in him, exempted from the ordinary laws which govern ordinary men. He is not liable for anything he may do. Whereas others would be, except for the crime that it is possible for him to commit - to make a mistake.

Now, obviously, any code which conferred upon an individual or upon a group extraordinary privileges without also putting on him extraordinary responsibility would be unfair and bad. Therefore, an Ubermensch is held to have committed a crime every time he errs in judgment, a mistake excusable in others.

But you may say that you have previously made mistakes, which I do not treat as crimes. This is true. To cite an example, the other night, you expressed the opinion and insisted that Marcus Aurelius Antonius was "practically the founder of stoicism," and in so doing, you committed a crime. But it was a slight crime, and I choose to forgive it. Similarly, I have and had before this matter reached - I don't know what the next word is - forgiven the crime which you committed or in committing the error in judgment which caused the whole train of events. I did not and do not wish to charge you with a crime, but I feel justified in using any of the consequences of your crime for which you were held responsible to my advantage. This and only this I did, so you see how careful you must be.

Now, Dick, just one more word to sum up. Supposing you fulfill both conditions necessary for reconciliation. One, waive claim to my statement, and two, state yourself that you no longer think me to have acted treacherously. We are going to be as good or better friends as before.

I want that to come about very much, but not at the expense of your thinking that I have backed down in any way from my stand, as I am sure of that in my mind and want you to be.

Well, Dick, the best of luck if I do not see you again, and thanks in advance for the wire I am sure you will be good enough to send. Hoping you will be able to decide in the way I obviously want.

I am.
Babe.
P.S. Excuse scrawl. Train is moving. Your spelling, young man, is abominable, and I, for

one, should advocate that Tommie-Boy be taken away from your instruction in the subject."

The final arguments took place on August 22, 1924, in an overcapacity-filled courtroom. Even the hallways were filled with hundreds of people trying to hear what was going on inside. Darrow took over twelve hours to present his summation, which mainly repeated the same two points in many various ways. One was that the boys had no self-control over their actions, and two was that they were still children, and therefore, shouldn't be put to death.

Darrow spent time attacking the death penalty itself rather than just focusing on the murder. He tried to emphasize that life in prison was a severe enough punishment as the pair would have the long day, months, and years ahead of them, which would seem like an endless road leading nowhere.

Here is an example of Darrow's flair for dramatics. By the time he had finished his statements, the judge was actually in tears. *"Tell me that you can visit the wrath of fate and chance and life and eternity upon a 19-year-old boy! If the state in which I live is not kinder, more humane, and more considerate than the mad act of these two boys, I am sorry I have lived so long."*

On the prosecution's side, Crowe had to bring the judge and the whole courtroom back to a sense of reality that these two were sadistic, brutal murderers. It was a significant feat to pull off, especially when you had a courtroom full of spectators, most of who, along with the judge, was still crying when he started his closing arguments.

Crowe had been frustrated to the point of anger throughout the trial, so he became very sarcastic in his attack of Darrow's closing arguments. Along with his sarcasm toward Darrow, he mentioned God as many times as he could, knowing that most of the observers were religious in their beliefs. *"My God, if one of them had a harelip, I suppose Darrow would want me to apologize for having them indicted."*

Crowe walked over to Leopold sitting at the defense table and looked him directly in the eyes before saying, *"I wonder now, Nathan, whether you think there is a God or not. I wonder whether you think it is a pure accident that this disciple of Nietzsche's philosophy dropped his glasses or whether it was an act of divine providence to visit upon your miserable carcasses the wrath of God."*

Crowe also referred to the alienists that

testified for the defense as the "Three Wise Men from the East." Crowe never referred to Leopold or Loeb by their names but instead always used derogatory terms such as "cowardly perverts," "snakes," "atheists," or "mad dogs." Crowe ended his closing arguments by demanding that Judge Caverly *"execute justice and righteousness in the land."*

After finding out about this next event, it really brought home how much things haven't changed at all. With fake news, conspiracies, and rumors running abound in today's world, just as they did back in 1924, this is something that could happen now.

On September 2, 1924, while Judge Caverly was in the middle of his deliberations on the final sentence to be given to Leopold and Loeb, he had to go into hiding. The media reported that he had been shot to death. Even the police believed it. In actuality, he was attending the funeral of one of his close friends. Mrs. Caverly stayed at their apartment located in the Edgewater Beach Hotel. While there, she received a phone call from Captain Roberts of the Chicago Police Department informing her that her husband had been shot to death as he was walking through the cemetery gates.

It turned out that Judge Caverly was fine. He was talking with a group of other attendees when she came screaming across the cemetery lawn to reach him. After he had heard what had happened, he had the phone line removed from their home. Several more officers were hired to stand watch and protect the Caverlys until the verdict was delivered.

I think the strangest part of this story is the capability of making the police Captain believe that Judge Caverly was shot. How did the rumor get to him? Why did he not check on the story with other officers before informing the Judge's wife? When it comes to the media, how could the newspapers and radio stations report on the Judge's murder without any verification? Maybe they got that from the misinformed Captain of the Chicago police.

SENTENCING

Even though most citizens who the *Chicago Daily Tribune* polled voted not to broadcast the trial on the radio, it was decided they would allow WGN radio to broadcast the last day of the trial. The sentencing was read because mainly the courthouse could only hold so many people, and literally, thousands wanted to see the trial and sentencing.

By the time the judge was ready to read his sentencing of Leopold and Loeb on the morning of September 10, 1924, the city had utterly stopped dead to hear it. Typically, you could hear the footsteps and voices of the people throughout the streets, but not on this morning. Throughout every office, store, and house, people gathered around their radios to hear the verdict.

A major sticking point for the judge, which took him two weeks to decide, was when Darrow pointed out that both Leopold and Loeb were not of the age of majority, which was twenty-one, and that the state had never sentenced any minor to death before. Nevertheless, Crowe was able to find a case of an eighteen-year-old that had been hanged several years before this trial and submit it to the judge as his argument for putting the pair to death.

Judge Caverly decided to hold back from executing both Leopold and Loeb. He considered it an extreme punishment for the defendants' age and instead gave them each ninety-nine years for the kidnapping offense and life for the murder. A significant statement that morning by the judge was, *"That it is within his province to decline to impose the sentence of death on persons who are not of full age. This determination appears to be in accordance with the progress of criminal law all over the world and with the dictates of enlightened humanity."*

As the press rushed to both the defense and prosecutions tables in the courthouse to get the attorney's statements, Leopold and Loeb shook Darrow's hand as they were taken away by the guards.

Darrow looked visibly shaken by the sentence. But he swept the hair out of his eyes and said in a normal tone, *"Well, it's just what we had asked for. It was the correct decision, even though it's pretty tough. This is far more of a punishment than death would have ever been."*

Crowe was visibly angry at the prosecution table, slamming books and papers around in front of him. He seemed far more concerned with his reputation than anything else when his first statement was, *"The State's Attorney's duty was fully performed. He is in no measure responsible for the decision of the court. The responsibility for that decision rests with the judge alone."* Crowe then grabbed what papers he could from the table, leaving others on the floor, and walked out of the court sternly, not saying another word to anyone.

Later that night, Crowe released an official statement to the press that read, *"Leopold and Loeb had the reputation of being immoral with degenerate behavior of the worst type. The evidence showed that both defendants are atheists and followers of Nietzschean doctrines believing that they are above the law, both the law of God and the law of man. It is unfortunate for the welfare of the community that they were not sentenced to death."*

Strangely enough, much later in Crowe's life, he had a change of heart about the death penalty. So much so that he even wrote a letter in support of Leopold's parole.

6

JAIL, DEATH & PAROLE

JAIL

Richard Loeb and Nathan Leopold were sent to the Joliet Penitentiary in Illinois, which allowed them to remain close and spend time together. Eventually, Leopold was sent to Statesville Prison in Illinois. It wasn't long before the two grew apart and even became angry with each other to the point where they started to blame each other for the situation they got themselves into. Loeb would also be transferred to Statesville, but by then, they were no longer friends.

DEATH

Loeb was slashed with a razor in the prison shower room by another inmate named James Day, who claimed that Loeb made sexual advances on him, so he had to defend himself. Loeb died later that night in the infirmary. Leopold was reported to be allowed to go to the hospital and spend Loeb's last minutes alive with him. Even though the prison guards who attended the fight between Day and Loeb said that Day had launched an unprovoked attack on Loeb and killed him deliberately, Day was acquitted of the murder charge.

June 1924
"Dearest Mompsie and Popsie.
This thing is all too terrible. I have thought and thought about it, and even now, I do not seem to be able to understand it. I just cannot seem to figure out how it all came about.
Of one thing I am certain, tho, and that is that I have no one to blame but myself. I am afraid that you two may try and put the blame upon your own shoulders, and I know that I alone am to blame. I never was frank with you - Mompsie and Popsie dear - and had you

suspected anything and came and talked to me, I would undoubtedly have denied everything and gone on just the same. Dr. Gluek says that I was bent on destroying myself, and I believe he was right. I seem to have discarded all the finer things of my life!

Mompsie and Popsie dear - it may seem terrible, but in one way, it is almost providential that I was caught. Going on that way, confiding in no one - there is no telling how far I might have gone. This way, at best, I have a long prison sentence staring at me, but I am hopeful that someday I shall be set free again, and I really and truly think that I shall be able to do some good and at least live a much better life than I would have been able to do otherwise.

I realize that there is always a chance of the death penalty. However, I am not worried, and I assure you that although I know, I never lived the part - I do know that should I pay the penalty, that I at least will die as becomes the son of such a wonderful father and mother as I know now more than ever that I have.

What I wanted to tell you is that I am not really so hardhearted as I am appearing. Of course, dearest ones, I am afraid that my heart is not what it should be, else how could I have done what I did?

JAIL, DEATH & PAROLE | 189

Dick"

Leopold ended up being a model prisoner with no issues after Loeb was killed. He became an X-Ray Technician for the prison hospital and spent all of his free time in the library reading and studying. In the 1940s, Leopold became a teacher in the prison school, where he taught prisoners to speak and write English correctly and some foreign languages. This led to him helping the prison create a new educational system to help educate all prisoners to be more capable of surviving the outside world when they got released from prison.

PAROLE FOR LEOPOLD

It started with a letter to the Parole Board.

Statement to the parole board by Nathan F. Leopold Jr.
  February 5, 1958
  "It is not possible to compress into a few minutes the thoughts and feelings of thirty-three

years, especially if those years have been spent in prison. For here, we have long hours to think, to think painfully, to regret bitterly, to repent fervently. A lot of those hours I have spent trying to understand how I could have possibly taken part in the horrible crime of which Richard Loeb and I were guilty. I cannot explain that even to myself. Maybe it cannot be explained satisfactorily, but I can give you a few facts and impressions which come out of my thinking.

I have been trying desperately to fathom this situation. I will never quit trying. I admired Richard Loeb extravagantly, beyond all bounds. I literally lived or died on his approval or disapproval. I would have done anything he asked, even when I knew he was wrong, even when I was revolted by what he suggested. And he wanted to do this terrible thing. Why…I cannot be sure. Certainly, it was mad, irrational. Maybe there was some kind of juvenile protest, ab overwhelming desire to show that he could do it and get away with it.

I had no desire to do this terrible thing. On the contrary, the idea was repugnant to me. For weeks and weeks, until only a day or two before the crime, I was sure we would never go through with it, that it was only something to talk about and plan but never actually carry out. Loeb made sure that we would actually do it. I could not stop him then. It was too late. I could not back out of the plan without being a quitter and without forfeiting Loeb's friendship. Hard as it is for me now to understand it, these, at nineteen, seemed more important to me at that time than a young boy's life. True, Loeb did the actual killing, but that does not exonerate me. Where were my moral instincts, my conscience?

The only thing that comes out of my thinking that even bears on it is that at nineteen, my growth and developments were unnatural; my thinking was of a grown person, but I had the feelings of an undeveloped infant. I was like an intelligent savage who knows no law but my own elementary desire.

In school, I had no trouble. I learned easily. I was several years ahead of the kids my age. I entered college at fifteen. The result was that I was always in the company of boys three or four years older than I. What a difference three or four years can make at that age! With school studies and the things you learn from books, I had no trouble. But what you learn from people - from your friends - I missed entirely.

You might say I skipped completely my early teens, and with that skip, I lost the growth *of character and the personality that normally goes with them. My emotions were at least five years behind my thinking. When they did finally catch up, which is not until I had been here in prison five years, I was shocked that I had not been able to feel things more deeply much earlier. Since that day, I have been able to live with others as well as myself.*

This does not explain much. I wish to God I could explain more, but it is all that has come of my long years of thinking about it. On the one hand, I admired Loeb, was attracted to him with the violence and lopsidedness only extreme youth can know. On the other hand, I missed the growth and development that takes place in the early teens; I did not have the moral strength and understanding to resist.

When my emotions did finally mature, when about twenty-five, remorse for what I had done set in and has never left me since, not for a single day. How can I hope to explain to you about that? To understand it, a man would have had to experience it, would have to have done something as horrible as I did, and repent it. You cannot possibly picture it. I cannot describe it.

Certainly, it is the strongest emotion I have ever had. It is with me constantly, sometimes in the front of my mind so that I can think of nothing else, but even when my mind is occupied with other problems, it is always there in the corner of my mind. It tinges my thinking all day, every day.

If you have stolen something, you can return it, or you can work to pay its owner back. Even if you have injured somebody physically, you can try somehow to make it up to him. But to participate in the death of a human life, what is there you can do? You cannot bring the victim back to life.

Gentlemen, it is not easy to live with murder on your conscience. The fact that you know you did not do the actual killing does not help. My punishment has not been light. I have spent over one-third of a century in prison. During that time, I have lost most of those who were near and dear to me. I never had an opportunity to say a prayer on their graves; I forfeited all home and family; forfeited all the chance of an honorable career. But the worst punishment comes from inside me. It is the torment of my own conscience. I can say that will be true for the rest of my days.

The only thing I have found in all these years that helped at all is to try to be useful to others. There are not many opportunities in prison to help other people. What few I have been able to find, I have seized eagerly- the prison correspondence school, for example, and the malaria project. To them, I have given my best effort. For it is when I have been able to be useful in a minor way that I have been happiest, or, at least, least unhappy.

One suggestion has been made that horrifies me - that if you order my release, I spend my time lecturing on juvenile delinquency or the causes of crime. I shudder at the thought. I am not an expert on anything. I will be lucky if I can make my own way if I am fortunate enough to be paroled. Certainly, I am not competent to lecture to others.

If I am fortunate enough to be released, all I want is to find some quiet spot with some organization where I can live quietly and modestly in an attempt to atone for my crime.

Nathan F. Leopold Jr."

After Leopold served thirty-four years in prison in 1958, he was released on parole. Shortly before his release in January of 1958, Leopold published his autobiography called *Life*

Plus 99. His book included his feelings about the kidnapping and murder of Bobby Franks and his relationship with Loeb.

Nathan Leopold, released from prison

You can still find copies of the book on Amazon and among other bookstores and eBay. After reading the book, I am not sure what I think about it. There are places in the book where Leopold writes like he is sincerely sorry for doing what he did to the Franks boy, but then goes on to say, "What's done is done," and that it's behind him now and there's no turning back.

He also claims that he still can't believe that he got involved in the crime and makes it sound as if he was talked into killing the Franks boy.

But throughout the testimony, we hear how he was a principal planner of the crime.

I also find it strange that he has to talk about being careful to act and do what ordinary people do and to stay one jump ahead of the police. If he is and was a truly innocent participant in the crime, why would he have to think like that? If he was truly talked into the plan designed by Loeb alone, he should be able to just act like himself.

When Leopold discussed Loeb, he made it sound like he didn't understand him, his wild mood changes, or sudden quick changes of mind. He made Loeb sound like he had this bright, cheery, magnetic personality that he couldn't resist, yet it would take all of Leopold's energy to try and stay around him.

Leopold talked about how Loeb thought he was much better than everyone else and constantly looked down on their classmates and friends. But it was Leopold who was heavily involved with the Nietzschism philosophy and believed himself to be an overlord, who introduced Loeb to the philosophy.

I also found it quite interesting that Leopold claimed to have been so in love with Loeb that he would try to emulate him in every mannerism, but if that were true, why did he direct Loeb in almost every place that the pair went?

Apparently, neither one of them cared much about the trial or being put in jail. They were both absent of emotion towards the sentence and only slightly relieved that they were not put to death. Leopold went on to say that deep down, he was hoping for a quick execution so the families hurt by the murder wouldn't suffer any longer, and it would be much easier for them than spending the rest of their lives in prison.

Yet when he talked about whether he had served a sufficient amount of time in prison for his crime, Leopold referred to everything he had lost while in prison, such as his family members who had died, the possibility of ever amounting to anything in life, and having a family.

Leopold claimed that the remorse he now felt only came from his time in prison. And that back when the crime happened, he felt nothing at all. At the time of writing his book, he called remorse his constant companion, and it has been with him for the last 23 years of his imprisonment.

Overall, it can be said that Leopold had no passion for committing any of the couple's crimes, and in fact, he only did the crimes and even the murder to please Loeb.

Leopold attempted to set up the Leopold Foundation to help emotionally disturbed kids who become delinquents and fund it from the royalties from his book. However, the parole board decided that it would be against his parole agreement and, therefore, he would be put back into prison, so it didn't happen.

In 1959, the movie *Compulsion* with star Orson Welles was released, which told the story of Leopold and Loeb's kidnapping and murder of Bobby Franks. The book of the same name had been released in October of 1956. This was before Leopold was released, and he thought the attention would be long over.

That same year, the Illinois parole board decided to allow Leopold to pursue his right to legal action and not violate his parole agreement. Leopold decided to sue the author Meyer Levin and the filmmakers Daryl F. Zanuck Productions for $1,405,000, claiming that both the movie and book were an invasion of his privacy, defamation of his character, and it profited from his life story. Eventually, the Illinois Supreme Court denied Leopold's claim because he was the confessed perpetrator of the crime and could not argue that any book or media production could injure his reputation.

The media attention became something

Leopold could no longer handle, so he moved to Puerto Rico. He earned his master's degree in mathematics and went on to teach. Leopold also volunteered his free time to help out in hospitals and churches. While there, he released the book *Checklist of Birds of Puerto Rico and the Virgin Islands*, which the University of Puerto Rico published in 1963.

Leopold met and married a widowed florist in Santurce, Puerto Rico. He had also developed diabetes, which eventually caused his heart attack on August 29, 1971. He died at the age of sixty-six.

PART IV

B-SIDE AND RARETIES

7

CHISEL BANDIT

This section of the book will give you some of the things I came across while researching for this book and the *Killer Queen* Series.

THE CHISEL BANDIT OF CHICAGO

I bet you are wondering why I am doing a chapter about the Chisel Bandit. Am I trying to get you interested in my next book? Perhaps there was a copycat killer in Chicago after the Bobby Franks murder and trial that used a similar M.O. to Leopold and Loeb? Well, actually, it's a no to all of those. Instead, this part is about something discovered while perusing the old 1924 *Chicago Tribune* newspapers for the Leopold and Loeb case. I learned about the "Chisel Bandit," whose notorious assaults occurred in Hyde Park and Woodlawn in 1922.

According to reports in the *Chicago Tribune* in September 1924, after the conviction and sentencing of both Leopold and Loeb for the kidnapping and murder of Bobby Franks, the trial State's Attorney of their case, Robert E. Crowe, said that he suspected Richard Loeb of being the "Chisel Bandit." When it was confirmed during the trial that Loeb and Leopold used a chisel wrapped with tape to kill Bobby Franks, Crowe decided to look into four other crimes committed using a chisel to murder the victims in those crimes.

The victims who were murdered included Freeman Louis Tracy, Melvin T. Wolf, and possibly a handless man found that was never identified. A fourth victim, Charles Ream, suffered a gland operation.

Later, it was discovered that during Richard Loeb's youth, he developed an affinity for experimenting on humans. He found that he could put people to sleep by using a chisel on them, and if he wrapped the chisel in tape, he could induce a concussion without cuts or fractures on his victim's skull.

He brought to Leopold's attention his clever way to knock out a victim so that they could rob them of their money and valuables. It was then that the pair set out on the dark streets in the Hyde Park vicinity to assault and steal from a chance passerby.

Leopold would step out from the dark and confront the victim by pushing his gun into their stomach. Loeb would then sneak up behind the person held at gunpoint by Leopold, and he would hit them on their head with the chisel. This method always gave Loeb a rush.

The pair didn't care if they obtained any money or valuables as that was not what they wanted from the attack. But they would remove anything they could find from the victim's pockets, such as fountain pens, pocket knives, matches, cigarettes, and cheap watches.

Several of these items were found in Leopold and Loeb's bedrooms during the Franks' murder investigation, but none had belonged to any of the Franks' family. They had little to no value to them, so at the time, they weren't important.

These attacks were probably their practice runs up until they committed the Franks kidnapping and murder. During that crime, Loeb struck Franks on his head several times, drawing blood to make sure that Franks was dead.

When the chisel used during the Bobby Franks murder case was later discovered, the other previous chisel murders were remembered by detectives. But there was no way to identify the culprits as the victims were considered inconsequential, and none of their families had even reported them missing to authorities.

Leopold and Loeb's defense attorney denied the claims and said that Bobby Franks was the pair's first and only murder. This argument seemed like an unusual way to defend your clients instead of showing evidence that it wouldn't have been possible for them to commit these crimes because they had some sort of alibi when these other chisel murders were happening.

8

LIFE AFTER DEATH

This chapter is dedicated to all the ghost hunters and paranormal adventurers that I have met, interviewed, or even worked with. Here you go!

One of the strangest things I discovered while researching this case was that Nathan Leopold wanted to know if there would be life after his death. If, by chance, he and Loeb were hanged for Franks' murder. Leopold was a self-described atheist even though he considered himself the apostle of true knowledge.

So, during the two-week deliberation time for Judge Cavalry to decide if their penalty would be execution or life in prison, Leopold came up with a strategy on how he would answer this question. His plan to find out what happened in death was not a new one. Others had already tried it several times before, or at least they attempted the method.

Simply put, the plan was that after his death by hanging, he would attempt to communicate from the other side a list of ten questions that he would create before he was hanged. The questions would be locked up in a vault and read only after his death.

After much thought, he had come up with the first draft of these ten questions and shared them with the press, knowing that he would alter them just before the actual time of his death. They would be read to friends of his choosing.

Here is the list of questions Leopold came up with:

1. Are the experiences of human life carried into the hereafter?
2. Is the intellectual or the spiritual the dominant note after death?
3. Is the absence of the physical being an advantage or a deterrent to such intellectual or spiritual happiness?
4. Is the hereafter dimensional as on Earth, or is there complete omniscience?

5. Does one retain reactions to the sensations registered on the mind previous to death?
6. Is life on Earth a necessary precedent to life hereafter? If so, how long a life?
7. If the intellectual is dominant in the hereafter, is Earthly knowledge adequate or insufficient to its enjoyment?
8. Is life on Earth a correct balance of rewards and penalties, or is there a higher judgment?
9. If life hereafter is spiritual, are the cultural experiences of the Earth necessary? What of the savage mind?
10. What is happiness?

My primary takeaway from this is how concerned Leopold was with what was more important – the spiritual or intellectual part of the being. Was he concerned that he had developed his intellectual being but had done very little work on his spiritual side? His questions centered around which side of our being is considered our happiness and which remains after death.

Leopold knew that he had the attention of

America because of the murder trial. Because of that focus, he had a better chance of succeeding than his predecessors, who also tried this experiment. Leopold pointed out that one such person to have attempted the same thing was Harvard psychologist William James, only he failed.

Another interesting point in this, especially after he wrote in his book, and I covered it in the previous section, was that Leopold claimed to have been talked into doing crimes, including the kidnapping and murder of Bobby Franks by his companion at the time Richard Loeb. Only when he spoke to the press about his possible upcoming experiment with the afterlife, he also declared that he was not afraid to die. His philosophy did not admit to fear and claimed that if he did have to face hanging, he intended on making a live speech just before he mounted the scaffold. He would not tell anybody what he would say, but he said that it would make the world listen. It sounded like even then, he lived through his ego. To add to this, Leopold, at the time of this report on September 3, 1924, just days before his sentencing, still believed that murder, under certain conditions, was not a crime.

Richard Loeb was taking this waiting period

to hear about the trial's outcome much more aggressively and was showing some anger. He didn't buy into the same philosophy as Leopold did, *"When I think of the long life down there (prison), I sometimes feel that it would be better to get it over with now! I don't care a damn whether I am hanged or not!"*

AFTERWORD

JOHN BOROWSKI | FILMMAKER/AUTHOR

A team of gay killers in Chicago. Just another day in the big city, right? I always say Chicago is the home of gangsters, serial killers, and corrupt politicians. But seriously, killers who are couples have been a part of the history of America, from Charles Starkweather and Caril Ann Fugate (The basis for the movie *Natural Born Killers*) to Doug Clark and Carol Bundy. Even though killer couple counterparts from other countries seem much more brutal, such as Fred and Rose West murdering one of their own children and Paul Bernardo and Karla Homolka raping and murdering Karla's own sister, during the late 1970s and early 1980s, Ottis Toole and Henry Lee Lucas were conducting their murderous rampage across the United States as they carried on their love affair.

There are similarities between all killer couples as far as there is usually a master and an apprentice, or a leader and a follower. In the case of Leopold and Loeb, both being males, the dominance seemed to shift from one to the other at times. Either way, they were both very interested in crime and pushing the envelope for the next thrill, placing them into the category of "Thrill Killers." Their fantasies escalated, and they always desired another thrill to top the last. We see this escalation in many serial killers. They had many fantasies, which ranged from sexual role play (playing drunk and play rape) to their fantasies of power, domination, and control over their victims. Many times, in gay relationships, when one falls in love, they can become blind as their feelings of love overpower their senses, especially during the 1920s when there were no outlets for homosexuals to relieve their sexual frustrations.

It is difficult to ascertain whether Leopold's ideals of the Nietzschean "superman/overman" were really true or if this was an excuse created for the court trial and sentencing. Many criminals have thought out their alibis and excuses, ready for a trial way ahead of time, and

AFTERWORD | 215

this shows in both Leopold and Loeb's meticulous planning of every aspect of the Franks murder, leading up to it, doing the deed, and then obtaining the money as ransom. Personally, I feel it is all B.S. as they were looking for a bigger thrill to top the last crime they committed. Thrill crimes are usually a build-up, starting with small, petty crimes and moving up to more heinous acts. Yes, Leopold and Loeb made up their own morality to justify their crimes. Later in the 20th century, crimes were blamed on video games, heavy metal music, and violent movies. But in the 1920s, there was not much to blame the violence on, other than dime novels and radio shows. Leopold wanted to please Loeb, and the passion of their sexual encounters was overwhelming in a society where their desires must remain hidden. For the entire 20th century, gays were outcasts, which was very painful. At the same time, the fact that gays were committing acts against the law by secretly seeing each other was very alluring.

I feel the bigger picture is the wealth and privilege which Leopold and Loeb were born into. In my opinion, this is the main reason why they felt they could do whatever they wanted, within or outside of the realms of the law. They both grew up in rich, prominent families and lived in the elite neighborhoods of Chicago. Their lack of morality was a guise for their privilege. But sometimes, the two can go hand in hand as some with money and power abuse their status as well as become bored and are always seeking a new "high." This makes total sense to me as their version of "living in the moment" can also mean committing crimes for thrills, knowing that they will most likely get away with the crimes due to their societal status. This view is similar to the attitude of the rich and privileged, that they can do whatever they want with no repercussions. I have seen this firsthand, and it does exist. Ultimately, the murder of Bobby Franks came down to the thrill and obtaining more money, which is never enough for the rich.

    The most fascinating aspect of the case comes down to the excellent detective work and forensic detection methods, considering this was 1920s America. The crime detection aspect of this case reminds me of how Albert Fish was apprehended by Detective William King and how the children's bodies were found by Detective Frank Geyer in the H.H. Holmes case. In the Leopold and Loeb case, tracking down the makers of the eyeglasses, tracing them to Leopold, matching the typewriter to the letter are all excellent examples of successful early forensics work.

Their blaming each other for the crimes once apprehended is typical of criminals who are involved in crimes together. The saying "There is no honor amongst thieves" is very true as criminals almost always turn on each other, as Leopold and Loeb did, bickering back and forth like children...or a couple involved in a relationship. After their numerous interviews, anyone would be confused as to who did exactly what to the Franks boy.

The trial illustrates how even any mention of being gay was salacious and controversial, as the attorneys were told they could whisper certain details about the acts of homosexuality committed by Leopold and Loeb. It seemed that Clarence Darrow is a hero to the gay community in his tireless fight to make sure the boys did not receive the death penalty. Yes, he was doing his job, but he was also defending the lives of these two young men in love. His closing speech, titled "I believe in the law of love," lasted seven hours.

I felt it was very interesting that the death penalty was sought for 18- and 19-year-olds, but it was the same with Jesse Pomeroy in 1874 when he was 14-years old. I appreciated the fact that the Judge dismissed the death penalty because of their young age, but specifically because there may be something to gain from studying Leopold and Loeb psychologically in the future. This is a reason I am against the death penalty as some criminals may be truthful, and as a society, we may be able to learn about them and their methods in hopes of stopping these types of crimes in the future. It is also very interesting that Leopold, upon his release, made the most of his life for himself and also for others, which is an excellent example of a prisoner rehabilitated, and his case should be studied by the prison system as an example of a rehabilitation that worked.

A big question of mine is: Why were Leopold's corneas removed and given to one man and one woman. Who were the people these were given to, and where are they now? I am sure murderabilia collectors would be very interested in those!

On a final note, I did want to address the fact that they were a gay couple committing these crimes. I feel their sexuality was important as gay couples ARE different from heterosexual couples. I remember a quote by the comedian Wanda Sykes, "We're different, but we're equal." And we are different. Being gay is an entire lifestyle, much different than heterosexual lives and relationships. Sure, there are similarities, but the differences are vast as far as upbringing, adolescence, teen years, and young adulthood. Growing up being attracted to the same sex brings scorn, bullying, and hatred from society and peers. True, some heterosexuals are bullied, but the shame and scorn brought down upon gays is different. Being gay automatically places the scarlet letter of hatred and discrimination on a man. I can just imagine how near impossible it was in the 1920s for gay men to secretly meet and have sexual encounters, but then if discovered, their lives would be a living hell, often ending in suicide. The time period, in combination with being gay, makes their relationship during the 1920s very different than a heterosexual couple.

TIMELINE OF EVENTS

Nathan Freudenthal Leopold born in Chicago, Illinois on November 19, 1904.

Richard Albert Loeb born in Chicago, Illinois on June 11, 1905.

Robert Franks is born on September 19, 1909.

Richard Loeb starts at the University High School at the age of 12 in 1917.

Nathan Leopold and Richard Loeb meet at the Harvard School for Boy in 1920.

Nathan Leopold's mother died in 1921.

Leopold and Loeb share a room together while attending the University of Michigan in the fall of 1921 and spring of 1922.

Leopold and Loeb start to plan a murder in November 1923.

Leopold writes the ransom note on his Underwood typewriter on May 20, 1924.

Leopold and Loeb kidnap Bobby Franks at about 5 p.m. on May 21, 1924.

Bobby Franks body is found by Tony Minke along with a pair of eyeglasses which would later find out to belong to Leopold.

Nathan Leopold was questioned by police on May 25, 1924, and again on May 29, 1924, both times at the States Attorney's office.

May 29, 1924: Nathan Leopold is picked up and brought into State Attorney Robert Crowe's office for further interrogation.

Both Leopold and Loeb were interrogated on May 30, 1924, by Chief Detective Michael Hughes.

Loeb Confessed to the murder of Bobby Franks early on May 31, 1924.

When Leopold heard that Loeb confessed earlier that day, he also confessed to his part of the murder of Bobby Franks on May 31, 1924.

Leopold and Loeb took detectives to where they had dumped the body of Franks, as well as Franks' clothing, the typewriter used for the ransom note on June 1 and June 2, 1924.

The trial against Leopold and Loeb began on July 5, 1924.

Leopold and Loeb both pleaded guilty on August 22, 1924, on the suggestion of their attorney Clarence Darrow.

Leopold and Loeb are both sentenced to life plus 99 years for kidnapping and murdering Bobby Franks on September 10, 1924.

Loeb is murdered in Statesville Prison, Joliet, Illinois by another prisoner on January 28, 1936.

Leopold is released from prison and placed on parole in 1958.

Leopold dies of heart issues due to his diabetes on August 21, 1971.

REFERENCES

ORIGINAL TRIAL DOCUMENTS & TRANSCRIPTS

1. Leopold's Confession Statement, May 31, 1924
2. Illinois Criminal Court Cook County Trial Transcript Leopold and Loeb I 1924 (first 508 pages)
3. Illinois. Criminal Court. Cook County. Trial Transcript Leopold and Loeb (pages 504-1089)
4. Illinois. Criminal Court. Cook County. Trial Transcript Leopold and Loeb (1090-1673)
5. Illinois. Criminal Court. Cook

County. Trial Transcript Leopold and Loeb (pages 1675 1924)
6. Illinois. Criminal Court. Cook County. Trial Transcript Leopold and Loeb (pages 2207 - 3023)
7. Illinois. Criminal Court. Cook County. Trial Transcript Leopold and Loeb 3024- 4411)
8. Penitentiary Mittimus - Criminal Court of Cook County (Sentencing) - Sept.1, 1924 - 3 pages
9. Psychiatric Review Leopold Impression While sick - June 30, 1924 - Dr. William Healy & Benjamin Bachrach - 29 pages
10. Psychiatric Examination of Loeb - 141 pages - Dr. Karl Bowman & Dr. S.H. Hulbert - June 24, 1924
11. Loeb Statement - Confession - May 31, 1924 - 32 pages

BOOKS, NEWSPAPER ARTICLES & OTHER SOURCES

1. "Letter with Death Threat Sent Father", Chicago Daily Tribune, May 23, 1924.
2. "Did you see Kidnapping of Robert

Franks?", Chicago Daily Tribune, May 23, 1924.
3. "Franks Inquest Awaits Report from Chemist "Chicago Daily Tribune, May 23,1924.
4. "Kidnapers' Ransom Note Shows Hand of Expert Letterer James Doherty," Chicago Daily Tribune, May 23,1924
5. "Collins Orders all Policemen to Look for Franks' Slayer," Chicago American, May 23, 1924
6. "Franks Death Letter Current Story in Magazine", Chicago Daily Tribune, May 23,1924.
7. "Kidnap Rich Boy", James Doherty, Chicago Daily Tribune, May 24, 1924.
8. "Franks Boy Gagged, Died Fighting," Chicago Herald and Examiner, Charles V. Slattery, May 24,1924.
9. "Experts Fix on Kind of Machine Kidnapper Used" James Doherty, Chicago Daily Tribune, May 24, 1924.
10. "Scene of Franks Crime", Chicago Daily Tribune, May 26, 1924.
11. "Question Woman in Franks

Murder," Chicago Daily Journal, May 26, 1924.
12. "Queries Race Theories Based on Boy Murder" Chicago Daily Tribune, May 26, 1924.
13. "Ransom Letter and Spectacles are Twin Clews", George Johnson, Chicago Daily Tribune, Page 2, May 31, 1924
14. "Franks' Case Suspects Upset by Chauffeur", George Johnson, Chicago Daily Tribune, Page 2, May 31, 1924.
15. "Richard Loeb as Best Friend, Letter's Theme" Chicago Daily Tribune, Page 3, May 31, 1924.
16. "Leopold Loeb Trial Opening Draws Nation's Interest", Chicago Daily Tribune, Page 3, July 21, 1924.
17. "Want Tribune to Radio the Franks Trial?", Chicago Daily Tribune, Page 2 & 3, July 21, 1924.
18. "Darrow Says Trial will Be in Cook County", Page 1, Chicago Daily Tribune Monday, July 21, 1924.
19. "Franks Hearing On Today", Chicago Daily Tribune, Monday, Headline Page 1, July 21, 1924.

20. "Change pf Plea Worries Franks Till He's Reassured", Chicago Daily Tribune, Page 2, July 22, 1924.
21. "Loeb Leader, Real Slayer, Alienists Say", Chicago Daily Tribune, Page 3, July 22, 1924.
22. "Call 100 Franks Witnesses" Genevieve Forbes, Chicago Daily Tribune, Headline Page 1, July 22, 1924.
23. "Crowe to Push Trial with All Possible Speed", Genevieve Forbes, Chicago Daily Tribune, Page 2, July 22, 1924.
24. "Trace chisel Crime as "D" in Loeb List", Chicago Tribune, September 2, 1924, Page 1.

ABOUT THE AUTHOR

Alan R. Warren has written several Best-selling True Crime books and has been one of the hosts and producer of the popular NBC news talk radio show *House of Mystery* which reviews True Crime, History, Science, Religion, Paranormal mysteries that we live with every day. From a darker, comedic and logical perspective, he has interviewed guests such as Robert Kennedy Jr., F. Lee Bailey, Aphrodite Jones, Marcia Clark, Nancy Grace, Dan Abrams and Jesse Ventura. The show is based in Seattle on KKNW 1150 AM and syndicated on the NBC network throughout the United States including on KCAA 106.5 FM Los Angeles/Riverside/Palm Springs, as well in Utah, New Mexico, and Arizona.

www.alanrwarren.com

ALSO BY ALAN R. WARREN

MURDER TIMES SIX: The True Story of the Wells Gray Park Murders

"The author even had me (who conducted the interview) on the edge of my seat as I was turning the pages as "the Detective" was trying to unearth the unspeakable truth."

It was a crime unlike anything seen in British Columbia. The horror of the "Wells Gray Murders" almost forty years ago transcends decades.

On August 2, 1982, three generations of a family set out on a camping trip – Bob and Jackie Johnson, their two daughters, Janet, 13 and Karen, 11, and Jackie's parents, George and Edith Bentley. A month later, the Johnson family car was found off a mountainside logging road near Wells Gray Park completely burned out. In the back seat were the incinerated remains of four adults, and in the trunk were the two girls.

But this was not just your average mass murder. It was much worse. Over time, some brutal details were revealed; however, most are still only known to the murderer, David Ennis (formerly Shearing). His crimes had far-reaching impacts on the family, community, and country. It still does today. Every time Shearing attempts freedom from the parole board, the grief is triggered as everyone is forced to relive the horrors once again.

Murder Times Six shines a spotlight on the crime that captured the attention of a nation, recounts the narrative of a complex police investigation, and discusses whether a convicted mass murderer should ever be allowed to leave the confines of an institution. Most importantly, it tells the story of one family forever changed.

JFK ASSASSINATION: THE HOUSE OF MYSTERY INTERVIEWS - VOLUME II

The House of Mystery Radio Show has been on the air for ten years, broadcasting in over a dozen cities in the U.S. It started as a way to interview guests knowledgeable in many of the world's mysteries involving crime, science, religion, history, paranormal, conspiracies, etc. The House of Mystery

Interview series is a curated collection of interviews from the show. Each volume focuses on one of the mysteries, providing the background and reproducing the main points discussed in the interviews. There will be no committed answer at the end, as the Interviews series does not attempt to solve the case. Instead, it provides the most compelling aspects of each theory held by different experts. This series is an excellent reference for researchers and a good overview for those unfamiliar with the case. Online links to the actual interviews are included.

Volume 2 of the Interview Series, "JFK Assassination," covers the unrivaled historical mystery of historical mysteries. The JFK assassination is the grandfather of all conspiracies in America and arguably where they all started. A highly popular President with movie star looks and charisma, effecting significant changes in society, was brutally cut down in his prime. The official story was that JFK was killed by a sole assassin, Lee Harvey Oswald. However, many conspiracy theorists believe in an assassination plot involving the FBI, CIA, U.S.

military, VP LBJ, Cuba's Fidel Castro, Russia's KGB, the Mafia, or some combination of those entities.

The research and interviewing of the JFK assassination experts lasted for over six years. Arguments and counter-arguments from a diverse mix of bestselling authors make for some interesting discussions. And some of the authors interviewed are considered just as controversial as the mystery itself.

Most authors focused on who they believe was responsible for the assassination. Others narrowed their focus on certain related aspects, such as the Zapruder film, Nix film, Garrison Tapes, etc. All information collected from each expert adds value to the overall mystery.

IN CHAINS: THE DANGEROUS WORLD OF HUMAN TRAFFICKING

Human trafficking is the trade of people for forced labor or sex. It also includes the illegal extraction of human organs and tissues. And it is an extremely ruthless and dangerous industry plaguing our world today.

Most believe human trafficking occurs in countries with no human rights legislation. This is a myth. All types of human trafficking are alive and well in most of the developed countries of the world like the United States, Canada, and the UK. It is estimated that $150 billion a year is generated in the forced labor industry alone. It is also believed that 21 million people are trapped in modern day slavery – exploited for sex, labor, or organs.

Most also believe since they live in a free country, there is built-in protection against such illegal practices. But for many, this is not the case.

Traffickers tend to focus on the most vulnerable in our society, but trafficking can happen to anyone. You will see how easy it can happen in the stories included in "In Chains."

DOOMSDAY CULTS: THE DEVIL'S HOSTAGES

Jim Jones convinced his 1000 followers they would all have to commit suicide since he was going to die. Shoko Asahara convinced his followers to release a weapon of mass destruction, the deadly sarin gas, on a Tokyo subway. The Order of the Solar Temple lured the rich and famous, including Princess Grace of Monaco, and convinced them to die a fiery death now on Earth to be reborn

on a better planet called Sirius. Charles Manson convinced his followers to kill, in an attempt to incite an apocalyptic race war.

These are a few of the doomsday cults examined in this book by bestselling author Alan R. Warren. Its focus is on cults whose destructive behavior was due in large part to their apocalyptic beliefs or doomsday movements. It includes details surrounding the massacres and a look into how their members became so brainwashed they committed unimaginable crimes at the command of their leader.

Usually, when we hear about these cults and their massacres, we ask ourselves how it possibly happened. We could also ask ourselves, what then is the difference between a cult and a religion? We once had a small group of people who unquestionably followed a person who believed he was the son of God. Two thousand years later, that following is one of the most recognized religions in the world. This book in no way criticizes believing in God. Rather, it examines how a social movement grows into a full religion and when it does not. And what makes the conventional faiths such as Christianity, Judaism,

Islam, and Hinduism stand above groups such as the Branch Davidians or Children of God.

www.ingramcontent.com/pod-product-compliance
Lightning Source LLC
Chambersburg PA
CBHW062056280426
43673CB00088B/487/J